D0840882

YOU
CAN HAVE
GREAT
SEX!

How the Nine Types of Lovers Find

Ecstasy, Fulfillment and Sexual Wellness

By Dr. Dennis Perman

PREFACE

Over the last twenty-seven years, I have coached thousands of doctors on all aspects of success, from business, to wellness, to communication skills, to inter- and intra-personal issues. I have seen millionaires made and broken, and heard every imaginable miracle and tragedy. But there is one challenge that seems to transcend talent, attitude, money, skill, and social status, one that affects literally everyone, which few have addressed and fewer have resolved. I'm talking about sex.

In my opinion, sex in our society is essentially broken. People like the idea of sex, and many wish for a good sex life. But due to cultural distortions and misinformation—and for most people, an introduction into their sexuality that is uneven at best, and traumatically miserable at worst—many don't enjoy it, most don't understand it, and almost no one feels especially comfortable with or well-equipped for it.

Yet, a satisfying love life is available for pretty much anyone who wants one, as long as there's a willingness to look at sex in a new way—not as one thing that is nearly impossible to figure out, but rather, from one of nine separate worldviews. This means that you can get clarity from your vantage point, instead of trying to apply only generalities. It is in this set of patterns that is uniquely you that you can find the kind of satisfaction that leads to a well sexuality. Each type contributes something special to the loving formula, and each looks at lovemaking in a particular way. It is through understanding the distinctions of your particular type that sexual wholeness, indeed, sexual wellness, is available.

Knowing which of these **Nine Types of Lovers** best describes you, and which best describes someone with whom you wish to have an intimate relationship, can make the difference between ecstasy and painful, frustrating failure. These ideas are that potent.

So, let me welcome you to a new way of experiencing yourself through sex; not the strained and incomprehensible old way, but rather, a revealing, embracing, attractive, and exciting new way—through the enneagram of sexuality. (Don't worry about this strange new word right now. It will be explained in detail later on.)

Before you begin to study this thrilling new material, please ask yourself two questions:

1. If there were no rules and I couldn't fail, what would my sex life be like?

2. Who would I have to be or become to have this sex life?

By the time you turn the last page of this book, you will have clear answers to these questions, and you'll be well on your way toward fulfillment in your love-making, regardless of your current status in relationship, self-esteem, or personal experience. This work is for you to awaken your sexuality—not in a dirty or vulgar way, but as a celebration of life.

You can have great sex. You deserve it. Put a smile on your face -- you're about to enter the world of sexual wellness.

Dennis Perman DC

Dennis Perman DC

Sexual Wellness Press
129 East Neck Road
Huntington, NY 11743
www.sexualwellnesspress.com

Editing by FirstEditing.com

Layout and Printing by BookBaby.com

Ordering Information:
Quantity sales. Special discounts are available on quantity purchases by corporations, associa-
tions, and others. For details, contact the Special Sales Department at the address above.

You Can Have Great Sex!/Dr. Dennis Perman—1st ed.

ISBN 978-0-9863977-6-9

TABLE OF CONTENTS

INTRODUCTION

"The key to true beauty is lots of water, great sex with Will Smith, and happiness. The key for me is I'm vocal about getting my happiness. Sometimes if you just say what you need then someone will give it to you." – Jada Pinkett Smith, <u>Redbook</u>, June 17, 2009

Most people want to have great sex—just ask them, they'll tell you.

The problem is, no one ever taught us how to do so, and even more challenging, each of us has a different perspective on what great sex means.

Some lovers like traditional man/woman sex in typical positions at typical times, while others prefer multiple partners, same-sex experiences, doing it in a public place, talking on the phone, or sheep.

While this may seem odd to you, you may seem just as odd to them. And further, it's almost impossible to know which type of lovemaking your partner likes until you find yourself in bed, either getting lucky with some successful screwing, or screwing it up.

Why isn't it easier, and how come no one has ever cracked the code of how to have more fun in bed and put it in understandable terms? This mystery is solved only when we begin to realize that each of us has a set of sexual patterns that is our definition of sexual fulfillment.

If you can tap into that formula for yourself, and recognize the patterns in sexuality that your partner (or partners) prefer, then the fog lifts. You can have the experiences you always wanted, and discover ecstasy in your own authentic way. Who you are determines how well what you do works, and it's no different in your most intimate moments.

The purpose of this book is to show you your patterns of sexuality, your directions to ecstasy, to help you learn to read such patterns in yourself and/or someone else, and to create your optimal sexual experience. This is true whether you are alone, with your lover, or in whatever configuration you desire—the end product is a life of sexual satisfaction, which I contend leads to a happier life overall. If you have more fun in bed, or wherever you want to make love, it relieves a multitude of other pressures, and helps you to face your other adversities with at least this one highly significant and rewarding piece of the puzzle in place.

Whereas most people grow up thinking there is only one kind of sex—the kind they like—it turns out that there are Nine Types of Lovers. This sounds more complicated than it actually is. Before you finish this book, you'll be able to quickly assess and understand which type you are, and almost as quickly understand how to relate to each of the other types when the situation arises. The patterns are unmistakable once you know what to look for. Armed with these distinctions, you can make love in a way that truly satisfies you and your partner (or partners.)

This is the pathway to sexual wellness. Your search may be coming to fruition, but the fun has just begun.

What Most People Don't Know About Sex

We are trained from the time we are young that there is one kind of lover. We see it on TV, read about it in magazines, and hear about it in hushed whispers on the street corner while growing up. If we have interests, tastes, or curiosities that differ, we are expected to be quiet about it—nice people just don't talk about that stuff. In fact, when we do, we are either ridiculed or ostracized, and that leads to the sexual repression that permeates even our freedom-oriented culture.

Parental input, however well-meaning, is often stilted and fearful, too uncomfortable for all but the most liberated adults to discuss freely with their children. Remember, your parents' sexual awareness, icky as it may feel to consider such a phenomenon (you got here somehow, you know), was based on their own limitations and reference experiences. These are biases that are difficult to transcend, and without information like that presented in this book, it was at best a crapshoot. Inquisitive kids are punished for doing the wrong things without getting a clear and objective explanation, and that leads to the distortions and generalizations that have paralyzed most of us sexually.

But you can demystify this complex issue and stop the trend of sexual confusion by incorporating some simple yet profound ideas. These will point your attention toward what works for you, instead of succumbing to the ordinary, the mysterious, the dull, or the whims of others.

You can develop a genuine, natural, and personalized appreciation for things sexual, and learn to apply what you know to attain heights of pleasure you may have thought beyond your reach. I can say this with certainty because the reason you may not have yet felt such sensations is that you weren't sure what to look for, or what it meant when you found it. This book will change that for you forever.

Nine Types of Lovers

You have your own way to experience yourself sexually, your own formula for sexual fulfillment. And while everyone has a slightly different description of sexual pleasure, people tend to fall into one of nine sets of behavior patterns, referred to as the **Nine Types of Lovers**. To begin to understand the **Nine Types of Lovers**, start by noticing that most people can be classified into one of three categories:

- people who lead with their **heart**
- people who lead with their **head**
- people who lead with their **body**

None is better or worse than any other, but they are different. And if you recognize your own patterns and those of your partner, it will save you endless distress and dissatisfaction, and show you a quicker and more satisfying way to fulfillment and wellness in your relationship.

If you are a **heart-centered lover**, then emotions play a major role in your definition of great sex. You will have feelings; supportive or unique, brilliant or dark. Or maybe you will avoid feelings because you perceive that they interfere with your ability to succeed, preferring to keep your experiences superficial so you don't feel too much. Heart-centered lovers often seek lovemaking that produces classical love; warm, heart-driven feelings, dramatic or tragic feelings, or outright avoidance of feelings while maintaining the façade of happiness.

If you are a **head-centered lover**, then you depend more on thinking than feeling. Mental pictures and self-talk are an important link between you and your sexuality. You may intellectualize your particular tastes or fetishes, study sexuality to become more expert at it, seek many experiences to avoid boredom, or just think constantly during sex. This robs you of some of the pleasure of being present in the moment while you are considering if you are doing it right, or wherever else your mind goes. These lovers often have elaborate definitions of pleasure that require a good fit, whether intellectual, insecure, or playful.

If you are a **body-centered lover**, then your sensations are most important to you -- not your emotions as much as your physicality, what you experience in your skin, and your own personal pleasure spots. These lovers are more likely to choose very pleasurable (or somewhat painful) lovemaking, or to avoid physicality because it feels uncontrollable, or somehow wrong to indulge.

You may already see yourself in these patterns. But not to worry if you don't—lots of details and distinctions are coming for you to be able to quickly place yourself in one of these categories. This will help make your lovemaking more satisfying, or get a better idea of what to look for (or develop) in a partner.

Each of these three basic groups has three subdivisions, leading to the **Nine Types of Lovers**. As you learn about each set of patterns, you will see where you fit in, and the answers to the riddle of your sexuality will be revealed to you. And when you add to that awareness the patterns of your lover, or apply them to finding and enjoying the kind (or kinds) of lover(s) you desire, the gateway to ecstasy will swing wide open for you to explode through.

It is important to note at this point that each type of lover is innately pursuing the same objective—sexual fulfillment through sexual wellness. It's just that each type has a different way of expressing and manifesting that desire. By recognizing and acting on the patterns that suit you best, you will find the great sex you always wanted, with the right person (or persons), for maximum enjoyment.

You'll notice that this book is arranged in two parts. First, we'll consider how relationship works, and how great lovemaking is created. In the second section, you'll learn how every type interacts with every other type, showing how every couple can have great sex.

We'll be exploring each individual type of lover thoroughly later on, but for now, we can't study sexual wellness without knowing what wellness is. Let's talk about **wellness—health and then some.**

CHAPTER ONE

Wellness—Health and Then Some

Ralph and Rebecca had it pretty good. Between the two of them, they brought in enough money to float their household, which is more than a lot of their neighbors could say. Their kids did okay in school, and managed to stay out of trouble. In fact, it was hard for Rebecca to put her finger on what was wrong, but it was clear to her that something was missing, and she could tell that Ralph knew it too.

She worried, is he losing interest in me? I try to do everything I can to make him happy, and he says all the right things. Why isn't it as exciting as it once was?

Rebecca would try to put those thoughts out of her head, but they came back to haunt her in her quiet times. What can I do to reclaim my man's attention? And what is he thinking? Is he really feeling what he says, that I still turn him on, that I'm the girl of his dreams? I want to believe him, and he's done nothing to make me doubt, but I just wonder if I'm being all I can be to him.

Ralph would wonder, too. He would wonder why Rebecca had to make things so complicated. Her mind is never quiet, he mused. She keeps second guessing herself. When she acts so insecure, it makes me anxious, too. I wish she would just chill out and go with the flow.

When he was tired of stressing over her constant overcerebration, he would settle into a comfortable reverie, dreaming of the two of them, alone on the beach, no one around, their nude bodies wrapped around each other, writhing in ecstasy. Not that such an event had ever happened, to be sure, but it made for an awesome fantasy, and he was willing to let that suffice in the absence of the real thing.

They did make love, of course—a slightly tense, walking on eggs kind of lovemaking that mostly led to forgettable orgasms and slight remorse and confusion. But he couldn't help recalling the old joke, "Hey, did I tell you about the worst sex I ever had? It was pretty good..." And so, he felt fortunate to have a willing partner, even if it was hard for her to stay present during the act. He was feeling it in his body while they were doing it, even if she was in her mind; and anyway, it was fun. And he loved the way she looked and felt, even if she never quite seemed okay about herself.

It wasn't unusual for him to crash afterward, spent, while she tossed and turned, longing for the romance she thought she signed up for. Rebecca, too, felt lucky, as Ralph was good to her, consistent and dependable, as long as she didn't require anything outside his normal routine. His predictability was somehow comforting to her, and she thought, I wouldn't put my card back in the deck and pick another one, before she drifted off into a fitful sleep.

Most people define wellness in terms of not feeling sick, but there is more to it. We all know people who seemed okay because they had nothing apparently wrong, and then boom! They die suddenly, of a heart attack or whatever. They may not have seemed sick, but were they healthy?

There's a difference between being well and having no symptoms, but most people aren't clear about this. Here's the way most people view their health, as if they are somewhere on a scale between sick and healthy:

Sick ⎯⎯⎯⎯⎯⎯⎯⎯⟶ Healthy

Depending on where they are on the scale, that's how they expect to feel. If they're closer to sick, they expect to feel bad, and if they're closer to healthy, they expect to feel good. Theoretically, this seems to make some sense.

But people's actual experience really doesn't follow this pattern at all. Most define their health in terms of the absence of symptoms, so their real options only go so far...

Sick⸻⸻⸻► Not sick

When you realize that health and wellness don't stop at the absence of symptoms, you see that there is another extension of the scale that opens the door of possibility, far beyond just feeling okay.

The Sexual Wellness Line™

Sick⸻⸻⸻► Not Sick/Healthy⸻⸻⸻► Well

Instead of settling for just not sick, you can deliberately choose constructive life management patterns that support you in going beyond, in many cases far beyond, just being not sick.

Wellness is a product of optimizing the factors surrounding your expression of health. Wellness is health and then some.

Sexual Wellness—Excellence and Intimacy

Sexual health and wellness are often misunderstood, largely because people tend to be uncomfortable studying, discussing, and discovering sex. There is considerable pressure on people to "know" about sex, to perform in a certain way, to be cool, to not be naïve or inexperienced, and that leads to a lot of self-deception and unclear communication. Though the intention is to not look foolish, which is completely justified, it shuts down the development of the beliefs, values, and habits that lead from sexual confusion to health, and ultimately to sexual wellness.

Most people, since they've been trained to settle for "not sick" with respect to other aspects of their health and wellness, usually settle in the same way sexually. If they're "not sick," they feel way ahead of the game. But there's a whole other side of the scale, which manifests when you are willing to look at sexuality as another branch of wellness that holds some of the most pleasure, fun, excitement, growth, vitality, and connection you could ever experience. You will find it truly worthwhile to learn to go beyond "not sick" through "healthy" to "well" in your sexuality.

It is that pathway that is the primary focus of this book, and the vision of this endeavor should be just as obvious—that as people apply the natural reasoning that they are accepting with respect to other aspects of their wellness, they will find that sexual wellness can also be attained. This is done through the gathering and assimilation of some simple distinctions, and the simple habits and behaviors that support them. Anyone, regardless of history, experience, or lack thereof, can be not only sexually healthy, but sexually well.

There are some general patterns of behavior that lay a foundation for sexual wellness, and then, it turns out that there are Nine Types of Lovers, nine different perspectives that shape each individual's and each couple's sexual experience.

If you understand your patterns and the patterns of your lover, you can catapult yourself to levels of unprecedented ecstasy.

If you ignore or abuse the patterns, you roll the dice, typically resulting in some blend of occasional satisfaction and frequent frustration, unfulfillment, dysfunction, and pain.

The good news is, you can learn these patterns, figure out your own sexual personality type, and start moving yourself in the direction of sexual wellness with a few simple observations and decisions. And when you learn your lover's type, you'll have a better insight into what he or she likes, wants, and needs in the intimate encounter to make it work better for both of you.

If a life of sexual enjoyment, consistent with your standards and values, and designed to create the optimal intimacy and connection with your lover appeals to you, then discovering your sexual personality as one of the **Nine Types of Lovers** can be your ticket to sexual wellness.

Patterns of Sexual Wellness

You will quickly learn that your definition of sexual wellness varies with your standards, experiences, values, and beliefs. That's why it's so important to identify the group of patterns that describes your type best, so you can have some foundational guidelines that are specifically relevant for you.

You'll understand yourself better, realize why certain things appeal to you while others don't, and get clear on what kind of sexual expression you prefer so you can move toward what you like and away from what you don't like. That kind of clarity lights the way for physical, mental, emotional, and spiritual happiness.

But before we delve too deeply into these highly unique tendencies, let's explore some of the general patterns that anyone can use to go beyond "not sexually sick" through "sexually healthy" all the way to "sexually well."

Sex can be playful. It can be intense. It can be familiar and rhythmic and mellow and comfortable, or exciting and spontaneous and wild and passionate. In fact, it can be all these things and more within a single lovemaking session.

But most of us have been trained away from detecting and interpreting our feelings in a healthy way, being misinformed about certain things being wrong, or dirty. Unfortunately, most of us got that information in hushed whispers, through distorted communications pathways (like the telephone game) or just making stuff up. It's the rare individual that even had any parental guidance on this at all, since so many are embarrassed to discuss it with anyone, including each other, much less with their kids.

So there's a vacuum, or at least an incompletion, where this intelligent and loving conversation about sexuality should be for most people. One of the purposes of this book is to begin or continue this conversation, so you can arrive at healthy patterns for yourself and have the most pleasure with the least pain in your intimate moments.

Points to Remember

1. There's a difference between being well and having no symptoms. Wellness is a product of optimizing the factors surrounding your expression of health. Wellness is health and then some.

2. If you understand your patterns and the patterns of your lover, you can catapult yourself to levels of unprecedented ecstasy. You can learn these patterns, figure out your own sexual personality type, and start moving yourself in the direction of sexual wellness.

Actions to Take

1. Lighten up on yourself. This topic of sexuality is really big for most people, so don't try to wrap your brain around every aspect of it all at once. Digest this information, get up close and personal with it, and let it develop, without forcing it.

2. Imagine how cool it would be to understand your patterns, and the patterns of a lover or someone you wish to be your lover. Think about how good it could be if sex was more accessible, instead of being so mysterious.

A Question to Ponder

Where are you on the Sexual Wellness Line?

(Don't worry, it's only your start point.)

The Sexual Wellness Line™

Sick————————▶ Not Sick/Healthy————————▶ Well

So, we've talked a little about wellness, and some of the basics of sexual wellness. Now it's time to discuss the next building block, the ability to create fulfilling relationships. Let's talk about **The Relation Equation.**

CHAPTER TWO

The Relation Equation

As the bus crunched to a halt in front of a large wooden ranch house, a man with a grey beard and gleaming blue eyes strolled toward them. As each couple climbed down, he greeted them as if they were already friends, with a wide smile, shaking hands, gently embracing some, and clapping others on the back with a familiarity that seemed, well, easy, even automatic. Ralph wondered how he made himself seem so kind and accessible so quickly, chalking it up to a smooth line and lots of experience. But he wondered if there was some trick to such immediate connection and charisma.

In fact, when Doc looked in Ralph's eyes, it was almost as if he were looking right into him. Ordinarily that would make Ralph feel invaded and uncomfortable, but not this time. "He is good," Ralph muttered to himself. "Real good. I have a lot to learn from this guy. It's almost like he gets me, even though he doesn't know me. How does he do that?"

The Relation Equation is the foundation of all relationship, of which your sexuality is a part.

There are two factors that combine to form every relationship, whether between lovers, parents and children, friends, employers and employees and customers, or whatever.

Why do you feel comfortable around some people, inspired or aroused around others, and repelled by others? It seems to us that our definition is based only on what the other individual is like. But it turns out that the interplay—the interaction between two or more people—is based on these two basic concepts. When applied, they will take this out of the realm of chance, and establish a series of guidelines that direct astute and effective relationship mates into a workable, loving, and if appropriate, even a thrilling relationship.

Developing Rapport—Connecting At Will

The first of these factors is known as *rapport*, defined as a bond, connection, or feeling of comfort. We've been hypnotized into thinking that liking someone is an emotional event, but oddly, it isn't—it's a neuro-mechanical event. Let's look at this strange word and see what it means.

The way that you perceive your environment, including everyone and every-thing in it, is dependent on your ability to interpret the input your brain and nerve system pick up. Your senses give you a conduit to experience the world around you, including your sight, hearing, touch, taste, and smell. These body functions stem from your brain and nerve system—the word *neuro* relates to nerve system.

The word *mechanical*, of course, means machine-like, automatic, unconscious, reflex, or involuntary. So the word neuro-mechanical means that your nerve system picks up certain input and has a typical, usual response to it.

That suggests that liking someone, or feeling connected to them, is based on reflex responses that come from the way your nerve system picks up and inter-prets what's going on. That's the reason why you can meet someone at a party and instantly feel "I like this person," or, "I don't like this person," though you may have little fact or detail to validate those impressions. It's an automatic feed-back system, and in most people who are unaware of this, an uncontrollable compulsion to feel good or not feel good around certain people.

The good news is, once you are aware of this tendency, you can choose or refine both the way you show up and the way you perceive those around you. You can learn to produce pleasing or connected experiences with people because you are noticing what makes them like they are, and how you can create a good feeling between you and them, based on a simple principle:

People who are like each other
tend to like each other,
and
people who are not like each other
tend to not like each other.
-- Anthony Robbins

So the first secret to generating the kind of connection that must precede the development of any quality relationship is the ability to cause someone to see you as *like them,* so they tend to *like you.* If they see you as *not like them,* they will tend to *not like you.*

Then, how can we willfully start this process of liking in motion?

Remember, the input your nerve system is seeking is sensory in nature, so the first key is to become sensitive to the way the other person is showing up, in other words, their tendencies and patterns—facial expressions, posture, movements, voice qualities like tempo or volume, word choice, those perceptible details that we mostly overlook, yet which hold a treasure trove of distinctions that allow us entry into the other person's world, with respect.

So, rapport begins when we are willing to detect the subtle signs that make someone uniquely them, so we can honor those patterns instead of ignoring them, like almost everyone else does.

This simple observation sets the stage for you to respond in a respectful, healthy, inviting way by doing something that may seem counter-intuitive. But once you understand it, it makes a lot of sense. The key is, you want to give the person back his or her own patterns, by *matching and mirroring* -- in other words, picking up their facial expression, posture, voice qualities and other characteristics, and reflecting those back to the other person. In this way, you are "like them," which makes them tend to "like you." This initiates a feeling of comfort, connection, and liking.

It sounds too simple, too good to be true. But to test it out, try this exercise with someone. You won't even have to explain it, just try it.

Rapport Exercise #1 (Connection)

Have a conversation with someone as you usually would, but see if you can notice how quickly or slowly they tend to talk. Deliberately speak at the same rate that they do. It will take a few attempts to get good at this, but everyone has the natural ability to do it, and you do, too. Notice what happens when you speak at the same rate they do. They will tend to smile, lean in slightly toward you, relax, most of what you might expect when someone likes you.

Now, vary the tempo of your talking, to make it faster or slower, and see what happens. They will tend to seem less connected to you, may lean away slightly, or lose their smile and sense of comfort. Then, shift back to their usual speed, and see them return to the more comfortable demeanor.

This may take a little practice, but within a few trials you will convince yourself that gaining rapport has nothing to do with someone's character, but rather is based on the neuro-mechanical patterns that either fit or don't fit. And a skillful and dedicated relationship mate can learn the typical patterns that feel good, and reproduce them willfully.

Match or mirror posture, facial expression, tempo of movement or speech, word choice, and breathing, and you can generate a deep connection with someone, at will, any time you choose. This works even with someone you do not yet know, or with whom you have no previous relationship.

As you become more adept at this easily learned skill, you will find that breathing patterns—rate, depth, location in the chest, and other subtleties—are among the most profound ways to connect with someone. (More about this later when we talk about how to create rapport with your lover in an intimate setting.) But first, let's explore the second factor that makes a relationship.

Commonality of Values—The Rules of Relationship

The second factor affecting the quality of your relationships is the ability to generate a commonality of values -- in other words, to establish the standards that are important to each other, and to communicate to find ways to support them for each other.

Notice that two people having an exact overlap on their values is unlikely, and that's why instead of talking about having the same values, we talk about generating a commonality of values. This simply means that two people know what's important to each other and are prepared to support each other in getting as close as possible to those important outcomes.

Another way to say this is that when we have rapport, we can clearly discuss what's important without friction or side issues distracting us, so we can come to agreement on the best course of action to meet both of our needs.

One of the toughest disconnections in relationship occurs when one mate erroneously believes that the other values something they really don't, or that the other hasn't shared what they themselves value. This is usually because it's never been discussed or communicated, but rather assumed. Such matters may start off as simply irritating, but if not addressed, often go beyond that. They may injure or end relationships that could have worked, or worked better, if only there was a more effective effort to explore the commonality and offer mutual support upon better understanding.

So, how do you generate commonality of values? Gain rapport by matching and mirroring, and invite the discussion with general questions about what's important. Talk about what's important to you about relationships, money, family, sex, or any topic either mate finds important. Only by communicating on these issues can you expect to get on the same page.

In rapport, it's less likely that there will be overreaction. But if one individual reveals something that is far outside the other's model of the world, it's better not to get crazy. Have a safe word or phrase, like: "Wow, let's not go there right now," or something like that, and revisit the topic after both have had a chance to think about it. It's much better to allow some time, and if the differences are indeed irreconcilable, how much better it is to know what you're dealing with, instead of the typical response of blame, judgment, anger, and misconception.

Most usually, though, the exercise leads to revelations that strengthen, enhance, and excite a relationship. Opening the door of possibility to new adventures, or giving insight into the way the other thinks, can be not only entertaining, but can provide significant building blocks to construct a stronger, better, more loving partnership.

Later, when we talk more specifically about the **Nine Types of Lovers**, you'll see how there are often patterns of values that can be predicted, investigated, and supported to improve the quality of your relationships. This is so not only in bed, but in every aspect of your life.

For now, it should be easy to appreciate that if one person has a high value on security, and the other has a high value on adventure, there will need to be some negotiation as to how that discrepancy is to be resolved. Likewise, if one values freedom and the other control, it requires a meeting of the minds to find the common ground. In extreme circumstances, there may not be a resolution. But knowing about the dynamic tension involved, and addressing it in rapport and with some determination to make it work, can create miracles in flexibility, self-acceptance, and love.

The Relation Equation can be conceptualized like this:

$$r + v = R$$
rapport + values = Relationship

Applying the Relation Equation

If you are in a relationship that is working, it's probably because you have a way of gaining and maintaining rapport. You have exchanged sufficient information about your values so that you have developed a reasonable commonality. Similarly, if your relationship isn't working, it's either because you've lost or haven't generated enough rapport to like being around each other and feel the connection. Or you have failed to support each other in key values that define each of your perspectives on the relationship—or both.

To test this, consider if the issue is based on a feeling of discomfort, or on a disagreement. The former occurs when rapport is violated; the latter when values are inconsistent. Either can lead to unhappiness. But remember—rapport is neuro-mechanical, so it can be restored by training yourself to match and mirror. This then gives you enough comfort around each other to test if there's a values conflict as well.

If there seems to be a values conflict, keep rapport by selecting a comfortable, unthreatening time and place to exchange ideas, and talk earnestly about whatever values seem to be out of harmony. Timeliness and lateness, neatness and sloppiness, money matters and sex, are frequent values that don't match up as well as they could. Be willing to get the cards on the table. Once again, preserve rapport by both parties being conscious of matching and mirroring, and you'll have the most productive and meaningful conversation on such matters you've ever had.

Using the Relation Equation in New Relationships

If you want to meet someone new and make a great first impression, remember to use your rapport skills of pace, posture, facial expression and voice qualities. You will cause the other to feel instantly comfortable around you by giving signals that you are like him or her. This instigates a feeling of connection that will not overcome a severe values conflict, but offers a chance to get closer faster, and come to that kind of discussion sooner.

Indeed, seduction is best executed in an environment of rapport, and clever pick-up artists become masters at this. That's why relationships aren't only based on rapport, but also the substance that accompanies a commonality of values. If you look at the Relation Equation, you see why some relationships hang in there though they may be somewhat deficient in either rapport or values. If there's ENOUGH rapport, meaning an unbreakable connection, then even values conflicts will not destroy the relationship. But it will render it ultimately unsatisfying for the one who suffers the conflict. Also, if there's ENOUGH commonality of values, like in a situation where the match is spiritually bound, even serious rapport violations won't destroy the relationship, though the likelihood of happiness, joy, and fun are remote, or occasional at best.

In other than such extreme cases, though, any two people who decide to have a fulfilling relationship can do so. You can learn to use rapport skills to match and mirror, and cause a bond or connection, and then elicit your values and your partner's values to compare notes on what's important. Then you can commit to supporting that, based on mutual understanding and agreement.

A Four-Step System to Relationship Formation

In 1965, a Princeton psychologist named Bruce Tuckman developed a four-stage model of group dynamics that has served as a foundation for team philosophy for the last fifty years. He said there were four stages of team formation—forming, storming, norming, and performing. Let's explore each of these stages in the context of the intimate relationship.

Forming is when the players on the team or the staff for a particular project are chosen. Forming is nothing more than assembling the relevant participants for the outcomes in mind. In the case of a newly forming intimate relationship, it would ordinarily be two people going through the early mating rituals to see if there's any chemistry whatsoever.

Storming begins when their values start coming to the surface. Generally, if there isn't sufficient rapport to get started, it never gets to storming. But if the two involved choose to take it to the next level, they must be willing to compare notes, and risk there being some conflict along the way. This storming process is where the rules and standards are discussed and agreed upon—or not, in which case the relationship doesn't flourish. Storming is essential to creating the boundaries of the relationship, so there can be a commonality of values—not necessarily the same values, but an agreement that defines what is tolerable and what is not from both points of view.

That leads to the third stage of *norming*, where those basic rules are put into play, tested, refined, and mastered. This is what leads to the fourth stage of *performing*, where the highly structured and rehearsed strategies of the first three stages are played out, in business, in academia, or in the bedroom.

Many couples stall in the storming phase, making it about the storm instead of the relationship. If you remember why you are storming, because you are involved in a process that leads to great sex, you may find yourself being more patient and more cooperative.

Rapport is essential, especially while forming, or else the couple never gets a shot. Values are elicited by storming, and commonality is developed when norming. And that's what leads to the kind of performing we all look forward to.

The Relation Equation and Sexual Wellness

When it comes to expressing your sexuality, especially if you intend to include someone else in the experience, the Relation Equation is a vital tool. Rapport skills give you an immediate and highly personalized technique of creating a feeling of connection and liking. Matching and mirroring initiates a physical bond that makes it more comfortable to touch, exchange pleasing facial expressions, and otherwise settle into a common groove.

Then, with that physical connection in gear, subtle and skillful elicitation of values hierarchies can provide a foundation for building a meaningful sexual relationship from the beginning—or, a realization that there can't be anything enduring there, which gives you the option of a fun one-night fling (if the values match up around that, of course). Or simply move on to someone else, depending on your outcome.

Working on your rapport skills will pay major dividends in satisfaction and fulfillment in a relationship. If you are engaged in a relationship, try this fun rapport exercise.

Rapport Exercise #2 (Intimacy)

Lie back to back, and take turns at this. First, one breathes at a certain depth and rate, and the other has to match to it, breathing at the same depth and rate. Then, when you feel yourselves coming into a rhythm, switch, and have the other start breathing at their preferred depth and rate, and the first now gets to match and mirror the second's breathing, until there is a synchronization.

You may notice several things. First, you may feel happy or at peace when you start to breathe together. This harmonious interaction would be soothing even if it didn't trigger a deep connection, but breathing rapport is some of the most powerful rapport you can get. When you match each other's breathing, it makes for a sensation of very close connection. No matter who initiates the depth and rate of breathing, when you breathe together, it feels good.

Second, you may realize that your preferred depth and rate of breathing are not necessarily the same as your relationship mate's. This explains why at times you lose rapport. You like each other enough based on the strength of your commonality of values to keep the relationship from going bad, but during "those times," it can never be as good as it could be if you knew when you were in and out of rapport, and what to do about it.

Lying back to back and practicing gaining rapport through breathing also brings your bodies into a shared balance and energy field, which many find to be a natural aphrodisiac. This feeling of connection may run very deep, and often seeks expression in sexual communion.

Notice, during your best lovemaking, you will naturally tend to breathe and move your bodies in unison, matching and mirroring. Now you can use this awareness deliberately, creating feelings of liking and attraction prior to bed-time, in foreplay, and especially in exploring new territory. This requires an open and honest connection to get clean responses and non-judgmental feedback.

Ralph and Rebecca made their way up the spiral staircase, and paused briefly before their door to face each other. Ralph always loved the way Rebecca looked, but he saw something special in her today, standing in the doorway with a quizzical smile. He smiled back, not knowing what to expect, but looking forward to trying the exercise.

"Well, let's give this a go," he said, and unceremoniously jumped onto the bed. Rebecca tentatively sat on the edge of the bed, looking slightly uncomfortable.

"What's wrong, honey?" Ralph asked, sitting up beside her.

"Oh, it's nothing, I guess," Rebecca replied, but he wasn't convinced. Ralph saw it as an opportunity to try on his newfound skills. He matched her facial expression, and reset his shoulders to resemble hers. Instantly, she seemed to relax, and he felt a better connection with her.

"Is there something you want to talk about?" Ralph asked.

"I suppose I'm just feeling weird. I saw you doing the exercise and getting rapport with Joanne and having a great time, and I think I felt a little jealous." Rebecca was shocked that she was able to verbalize her concerns so easily.

Ralph laughed. "You have nothing to worry about, Rebecca. You have always been the only one for me. I love you, and nothing can ever change that. Why don't we do our exercise and get back to the room to share with the others about being able to have such a difficult conversation so gracefully. If it's okay with you, that is, I just think it would help the others, too."

Rebecca melted into his arms. "I love you too, Ralph. Thanks for being so good to me." They snuggled into the bed, facing away from each other, just as Doc Rogers recommended.

At first, lying back to back felt strange. They were touching, but felt somehow disconnected, and Ralph realized that Rebecca was breathing very quickly, while he was breathing more slowly and deeply. Ralph said, "I'll go first," and adjusted his breathing rate and depth to be more like Rebecca's, quicker and shallower, and higher in the chest.

Ralph was amazed. Just that small shift created an instantaneous wash of comfortable sensations throughout his body, and he could tell that Rebecca felt it too, as a small moan of pleasure escaped her lips.

"Did you feel that?" Ralph wanted to make sure he hadn't hallucinated the new feelings.

"Yes, Ralph, I did, it was amazing," Rebecca enthused. "Just a few moments ago I felt so uncomfortable, and now, it just feels good. Can I try it too?"

"Sure," said Ralph. They both went back to their more natural rate and depth of breathing, and this time, Rebecca slowed her pace

and deepened her rhythm. And this time, something very special happened.

As they lay back to back, breathing together, both started to feel a stirring inside themselves that could only be interpreted as... wanting each other. Ralph turned around to see Rebecca's eyelids heavy, her breathing slow and deep, her lips parted. He could not resist her. He kissed her, and their tongues swirled. His fingers stroked her cheek, tracing the curve of her neck with the tips. Slowly, lovingly, he skimmed her shoulder, making her tremble with anticipation, and he ran his hands gently over her back, squeezing her butt lovingly, pulling her closer to him.

They looked into each other's eyes, with a different kind of lust than they were used to. Not a horny, ravenous feeling, but rather a graceful, naturally right desire that could only culminate in their union.

They undressed quickly and returned to each others' arms, still breathing together, still touching each other sensitively. He grazed his hand over her breasts, and she gasped with delight. She ran her nails down his back and then up his thighs, touching him in a way he longed for but she rarely did.

Both reaching the height of arousal, they could not delay. Resistance was futile, and they moved together in beautiful harmony, cantering rhythmically, building to a full gallop, and then coming together in an explosion of ecstasy.

They were silent for a few minutes, and then Ralph uttered the only relevant syllable he could think of. "Wow," he said.

"Wow is right! Ralph, you're amazing!" Rebecca gushed. "That was, like, the best ever!"

"You mean the best yet, my darling." Ralph smiled.

Prospecting With the Relation Equation

Needless to say, if using rapport skills, matching smiles, postures, movements, word choice, or voice qualities can create a bond between those who already have a relationship, it's equally valuable for those who wish to initiate one, whether long or short term. And remember, your values are yours to decide upon. It only creates problems when you don't stop to consider the other person's values in the equation.

Finding someone with whom you can gain rapport, whose values dovetail with yours, can be the answer to your relationship question for life. Some people want a monogamous relationship, some want more than one or many relationships. Some prefer particular ethnicities or age groups, some like opposite or same sex, some prefer specific physical characteristics like blond or muscular, and every imaginable combination. But armed with The Relation Equation, you can make a connection with anyone you want to. Once you refine and master your rapport skills, and you can elicit their values and share yours to discover the suitability and fit, both of you will know your best course of action.

Sexual wellness is not just about great sex, though it includes it. Sexual wellness means deliberately choosing habits, behaviors, beliefs, and values that are consistent with your best possible sexual expression. This will provide optimal satisfaction based on your formula for fun and fulfillment -- your directions to ecstasy.

Adventure? Love? Warmth? Security? Talking sweet talk? Talking small talk? Talking dirty? Not talking at all? Everyone has a different hierarchy of desire, and no one ever taught us how to communicate it to each other. We became dependent on being good guessers instead of attentive and committed lovers. But now you will have an alternative that can be learned and mastered with a little effort and perseverance.

I remember that I first learned this simple technique at the old Anthony Robbins seminar called "The Mind Revolution," which evolved into the extraordinary "Unleash The Power Within!" seminar. After gaining rapport, simply ask the question, "What's important to you..." and then finish the question with the topic you want to talk about. For example you could ask, "What's important to you in a relationship?" Or, you could chunk down and ask, "What's important to you in a conversation?" Or, you could chunk up and ask, "What's important to you in a lifetime partner?" You see, you can adjust the scope of the question, but by engaging in a series of conversations like this, you construct a clear idea of the other person's model of relationship.

While this approach is useful in any relationship, it's especially relevant and useful in the context of the sexual relationship. Part of moving toward sexual wellness is learning to talk honestly and intelligently about your desires, fears, expectations, and rules. Your underlying values and beliefs and the resource states you have available to work with form a backdrop for your behaviors, essentially determining which habits and behavior patterns you will typically default to.

But you don't have to settle for the tendencies. You can learn to circumvent or even transcend your limiting patterns by being aware of them and breaking them when you notice them. That's how new habits are formed—catching yourself in the disempowering pattern, and consciously replacing it with your new desirable pattern, until it is conditioned and happens as a new reflex.

So, if you notice that on The Sexual Wellness Line™ you are starting to the left of the "not sick" marker, you may have some healing and reframing to look forward to before you can claim to be truly well sexually. Good news, though— almost anyone can move in a positive direction quickly and steadily, as long as you are willing to let go of the past and look forward to a better future.

NLP and Sexual Wellness

I mentioned Tony Robbins, one of my mentors, and one of the world's great masters of personal growth technology. Among many useful distinctions he has shared with his students over the years, he brought cultural attention to a previously little-known science—neurolinguistic programming, or NLP for short.

NLP studies human excellence, and measures and quantizes it so it can be duplicated and reproduced. It is based on an exploration of how what we think and communicate, both to ourselves and others, affects our patterns of behavior and emotion. If you can understand thoroughly how someone creates a beneficial behavior pattern, then you can learn to reproduce it and reap the benefits of that behavior. Further, if you can solve the riddle of a disempowering pattern, you can learn to break that habit and condition a better one.

Using simple building blocks based on the senses—what you see, hear, and feel—you can figure out the formula for your best habits and behavior patterns. This allows you to perform at your best, and train others to do the same.

You can easily see how this could be useful in the bedroom. If you know someone appreciates input visually, then how you and they look will be important to them, as well as the lighting and the appearance of the room. If what you hear is important, the choice of music, sultry whispers, or periods of silence might play a big part in creating the experience you prefer. When feelings are paramount, then how you touch, when you touch, and where you touch are the determining factors for the desired effect. And unless you find out your partner's patterns, you're guessing, and your chances of effective interaction are reduced.

Tools like matching and mirroring to gain rapport, asking questions to develop commonality of values, and recognizing the tendency to be more visual, more auditory, or more kinesthetic, are general patterns that apply to all Nine Types of Lovers. If you did nothing more than gain and maintain rapport, support each other's values, and observe a few guidelines about general approach, your lovemaking would be that much better.

Points to Remember

1. All relationships require two components—the ability to gain rapport, and the ability to generate a commonality of values.

$$r + v = R$$
rapport + values = Relationship

2. Tools like matching and mirroring to gain rapport, asking questions to develop commonality of values, and recognizing the tendency to be more visual, more auditory, or more kinesthetic, are general patterns that apply to all Nine Types of Lovers.

Actions to Take

1. During a conversation, vary your speed, and notice when you feel comfortable, and when the other party seems comfortable. You are good at this already; notice while you are doing it!

2. Ask someone about their values. For example, ask, "What's important to you about ___?" and get some experience asking such questions and listening to and interpreting the answers. You'll get to know the other person well, they'll feel respected and admired, and you'll develop your communication skills.

A Question to Ponder

Which do you think you are naturally better at: gaining rapport with someone, or eliciting their values by asking good questions?

With the cornerstones of sexual wellness and the Relation Equation in place, we can begin to explore the nuances and fascinating flavors of quality lovemaking. Now, it's time to look deeply into the eyes of sexuality, and see the **Nine Facets of Sexual Expression** that are illustrated by the **Nine Types of Lovers**.

CHAPTER THREE

Nine Facets of Sexual Expression

Everyone does it, you know that's okay
We like it how we like it, our very own way
We all want to feel we're connecting through love
But most of us don't get to feel it enough

You surely intend to make someone feel good
But you don't always do what they're wishing you would
And you want something more, though you love 'em to death
What's missing is simple, it's called Triple F.

Triple F is a Formula for Fun and Fulfillment
It means no more wondering where all the thrill went
So open your hearts, and your bodies and minds
There's Nine Types of Lovers, you're one of those kinds.

Each of us tends to use typical patterns
That's the way everyday lovemaking happens
Strange as it seems, some will lead with their head
Their thinking is part of their thriving in bed

But some people, rather, are more body-driven
Running on instincts they sense are God-given
Still other people are led by their hearts
It's in their emotions relationship starts

The heart-driven lovers are Givers and Stars,
And also Romantics, heart-centered they are
Professors and Thinkers will lead with their minds
And also the Players are head-centered kinds

Dominants tend to be powerfully strong
While Dreamers are pleasantly coasting along
Elegants also are body-led lovers
Which type you are you're about to discover

Soon you'll be swept up in sexual trance
Where your minds, hearts and bodies will whirl into dance
And you'll learn to respond to your innermost urging
Where love's overwhelming and pleasure keeps surging

It all comes from knowing your sexual type
To cut through the misinformation and hype
To be who you really are, pure, clean and true
And be with your lover, authentically you

There's a wonderful wellspring of passion inside you
And you can experience it when you decide to
A wellspring of passion, awaiting expression
The world's greatest sex every lovemaking session

Looking at love one of nine different ways
Is a sex revolution, and you'll be amazed
That realization's about to break through
Nine Types of Lovers, so which one are you?

Givers are loving, supportive and kind
Stars need to look like the best all of the time
Romantics are sensitive, self-absorbed, tragic
Professors prefer understanding the magic
Thinkers are insecure, questioning all
Players love newness and having a ball
Dominants claim their control with their strength
Dreamers can fantasize to any length
Elegants like when we follow the rules
Nine Types of Lovers, which one are you?

One of the types has your signature on it
It will appear as you focus upon it
Please make distinctions till only one's left
And that is the way you'll achieve Triple F!

And don't forget it's for your partner as well
To magnify pleasure and thrill every cell
Sexual ecstasy beyond compare
That is the joy behind Triple F Squared!

There's a wonderful wellspring of passion inside you
And you can experience it when you decide to
A wellspring of passion, awaiting expression
The world's greatest sex every lovemaking session

Looking at love one of nine different ways
Is a sex revolution, and you'll be amazed
That realization's about to break through
Nine Types of Lovers, Nine Types of Lovers
Nine Types of Lovers, so which one are you?[1]

Sex is a creative process. It starts someplace, goes someplace, and ends someplace. The way you represent your sexual beliefs, values, feelings, and desires is unique to you, one of a kind, and unlike anyone else. But each of us follows some patterns of behavior, and when we see them, it can help us understand how to feel happier and more fulfilled in our sex life.

There are nine qualities that tend to be really important to us sexually, called the **Nine Facets of Sexual Expression**. Each of these is a portal into one of nine sexual personality types. By understanding the Nine Facets and recognizing which you relate to most, you can begin to identify your type.

The net impact of this understanding and application is that you begin to experience a sense of fulfillment, as well as fun. Often sex is fun; I mean, it's better than a sharp stick in the eye. But to be both fun and fulfilling, for it to be really great sex, there is a particular formula, unique to each of us, which can be

---

1 *To download the "Nine Types Of Lovers" song, go to www.YouCanHaveGreatSex.com/NineTypesOfLovers/songs*

identified and used to create the optimal environment. This is called **Triple F**, which stands for the **Fun-Fulfillment Formula**.

Triple F is your personal design of the very best sex possible. Everyone has their own formula, and when you think about it, this is something you want your lover to know about. It can avoid what you don't like, and invite more of what you do like.

Notice that your partner is in exactly the same predicament. He or she has a personal formula as well, and the rules hold in reverse, too. He or she would do better if you knew the definition of sexual fulfillment for your partner, so he or she can also get to **Triple F.**

When both partners are at **Triple F**, that's called **Triple F Squared**, a launching pad for ecstasy, and a necessary precondition for maximizing sexual wellness. Both partners acting on and receiving their own formula for great sex is likely to produce great sex, by your own definition. And when that happens consistently, that is sexual wellness.

So, sexuality is not one thing. It has many shapes, sizes, and colors, with many ways ecstasy and fulfillment can be attained. You could categorize these myriad intricacies of desire into nine groups, which define the **Nine Facets of Sexual Expression.**

Here are the Nine Facets:

Love: Considered the most attractive force known, love is actually one of nine key elements that make up your optimal sexuality. In this group, we include both affection and kindness, as well as support and willingness to be available to a partner's desires.

Growth: A sexual relationship is a living, thriving confluence of energies that must keep growing and evolving to remain vital. Personal development and learning are essential to growth, as is creating sexual intentions and following through on them.

Beauty: Seeing what is beautiful in yourself, your partner, and the two of you together is a critical aspect of sexuality. Being appealing to your partner and feeling enticed by him or her is an important piece of sexual wellness. Uniqueness and individuality also play a role here, in liberating you from the preconceived notion of what is beautiful as dictated by cultural norms. Each of us has our own special something, and noticing that is part of the facet of beauty.

Wisdom: Knowing how relationships work and how sexuality is optimized requires insight, knowledge, and perspective. Both an awareness of the mechanics of lovemaking and a deeper insight into the essence of relationship bring wisdom into sexuality.

Security: Feeling safe and certain is a necessary precondition to opening up as a lover to a lover, and trusting that the sanctity of the relationship will be preserved, as defined by those involved, will deliver a sense of security. The underbelly of this is overcerebration, which breeds fear and doubt. But along with this facet comes responsibility, upon which security depends, and from which the relationship is stabilized.

Passion: Relationships need excitement, enthusiasm, variety, and spontaneity to stay fresh and compelling. Fun, happiness, adventure, curiosity, and lust are part of the passion group.

Strength: Power to lead and power to protect are keys to a solid relationship, and sexually this often takes the form of dominance, or at least control. Turned up too high it might look like bullying, but strength is needed to hold tight during turbulent times, and sometimes to choose direction and guide when the other partner is stuck.

Harmony: Peaceful coexistence and the ability to mediate and resolve conflict are vital to a thriving relationship. And just as much sexually, being able to stay calm and centered in times of adversity or plenty, balances and steadies the relationship.

Fidelity: Having a code of conduct and a rules structure that both mates recognize and uphold sets the stage for ideal order and consistency, and reduces the likelihood of unfaithfulness or other transgressions.

You'll observe that we all have all of these facets to varying degrees and in different proportions. That's what adds color and personality to the Nine Types. One of these will come to the forefront for each of you, and that is a gateway to understanding your type. But each of us has uniquely blended these attributes, which gives us our own personalized viewpoint on sex.

Whether it jumps out at you and seems obvious right away, or takes a while for you to conclude which of these facets is most prevalent for you, you will ultimately see how this pathway and the patterns that grow out of it are a wormhole to another dimension, where people are sexually well, happy, and fulfilled.

You can be one of them. You can have great sex, and these distinctions will help you get there.

Points to Remember

1. There is a particular formula, unique to each of us, which can be identified and used to create the optimal environment. **Triple F** stands for the **Fun-Fulfillment Formula**. **Triple F** is your personal design of the very best sex possible.

2. When both partners are at **Triple F**, that's called **Triple F Squared**, a launching pad for ecstasy, and a necessary precondition for maximizing sexual wellness.

3. There are Nine Facets of Sexual Expression: Love, Growth, Beauty, Wisdom, Security, Passion, Strength, Harmony, and Fidelity.

Actions to Take

1. Think of various people you know, and see if you can match up their personality (as you know them) with one of these facets of sexual expression.

2. Try on each of these facets, considering what it means to you, and how relatively important it is to you. There's no right or wrong, just what do you think about each?

A Question to Ponder

Does one of these facets stand out for you personally more than any of the others?

Now, we're ready to see how these Nine Facets lead to the **Nine Types of Lovers**.

CHAPTER FOUR

The Three Basic Love Styles

Each of us tends to use typical patterns
That's the way everyday lovemaking happens
Strange as it seems, some will lead with their head
Their thinking is part of their thriving in bed

But some people, rather, are more body-driven
Running on instincts they sense are God-given
Still other people are led by their hearts
It's in their emotions relationship starts.

There are three basic love styles—heart, head, and body. Heart-centered lovers, head-centered lovers, and body-centered lovers have different patterns. Each of the three has three subdivisions that give us the **Nine Types of Lovers.**

Let's talk about each of the three basic love styles, and the three types in each category.

Heart-Centered Lovers:
Givers, Stars, and Romantics

Heart-centered lovers are driven by their emotions. They want to feel good ones, to feel unique ones, or to avoid feeling altogether so they don't get distracted from other things that are important to them.

Some heart-centered lovers give to the point that they may lose themselves in their giving. Before you judge that, for them it may be just what they want. Some prefer the drama or darkness of painful or unrequited love. Once again, try not to think of this as right or wrong, but rather recognize that each of us has beliefs, values, and life experiences that lead us to feel a certain way. This discussion is more about understanding than judgment.

Some heart-centered lovers do their best to stay out of their hearts, choosing instead to keep love superficial, either to prevent unnecessary pain, or to keep sex at a distance so they are not commandeered by it. They may excel at other non-sexual endeavors, and opt to feel less to achieve more, which often shows up as shallowness, an "absence" of heart.

People who lead with their hearts are often vulnerable, which explains why some make themselves very available sexually, and others make themselves considerably less so. Their hearts would tend to be wide open if they didn't watch out. Of these three types, one wants to open their heart, one wants to open it only under certain circumstances, and one wants to keep it closed.

Head-Centered Lovers:
Professors, Thinkers, and Players

Head-centered lovers are driven by their thoughts. Thinking is different from feeling in that it is more easily measured, quantized, and analyzed. Mental processes like visualization and self-talk play a major role for head-centered lovers. This can be very good, as language can be used to describe what feels good and what doesn't. And, it can be not so good, as rational thought often turns out to be inadequate in fully expressing feelings.

So, since head-centered lovers depend more on thinking than feeling, mental pictures and inner voices are an important link between them and their sexuality. They may ponder or experiment with particular tastes or fetishes, study sexuality to become more expert at it, seek many experiences to avoid boredom, or just think constantly during sex, which takes them out of the feelings of the present moment.

Body-Centered Lovers:
Dominants, Dreamers, and Elegants

Body-centered lovers have their pleasure centers in their bodies. They are very physically oriented, enjoying sensations and rushes of pleasure, or allowing only certain sensations while others are avoided or hidden.

Where heart-centered lovers get their power from their feelings, and head-centered lovers get their power from the thoughts, body-centered lovers get their power from their instincts. So rather than being driven by their thoughts or feelings, they respond to their gut feel, an inner sense of how things are.

Body-centered lovers may control their bodies, engage their bodies, or repress their bodies. Those who retain control may be very physical or not, preferring to control their desires as a demonstration of power. Those who engage their bodies really lose themselves in lovemaking, while those who repress their bodies often deny themselves the satisfaction of sexual release, thinking it improper.

Remember that there are some general patterns that transcend type. All types of lovers must be able to gain and maintain rapport. All types of lovers must be able to establish a commonality of values. All types must notice if they are more visual, more auditory, or more kinesthetic. And all types must pursue their own individual recipe for their Triple F. Their partner must do the same, so that they can compare notes and derive the very best combination possible. If you want to have great sex, this is the shortest distance between two points.

Once you have built this firm foundation, the unique blueprint for your best lovemaking can be constructed; lovingly, passionately, and precisely as both of you wish. It's worth the investment, especially since the experimentation as you strive together to figure out the optimal patterns of behavior is a direct route to Triple F.

Think about it—you'll be trying on different sexual practices and habits to see which seem best. Doesn't that sound like a good time? Even the behaviors that don't work will be entertaining, and they'll only reinforce the stuff you do like. That's how to get to Triple F. And when you do it together, the necessary climax is Triple F Squared.

Points to Remember

1. There are three basic love styles—heart-centered, head-centered, and body-centered.

2. Heart-centered types are Givers, Stars, and Romantics. Head-centered types are Professors, Thinkers, and Players. Body-centered types are Dominants, Dreamers, and Elegants.

Actions to Take

1. Think about what it might be like to be in an intimate encounter with someone you find attractive. Do you find yourself thinking, getting emotional, or feeling it in your body?

2. Consider if any of the types of lovers described here are definitely not you. That's one way to narrow down the options to begin to discover your type.

A Question to Ponder

Do you recognize yourself yet in one of these basic love styles?

Now, let's dig a little deeper into each type. First let's take a closer look at each of the three types of heart-centered lovers, and see how they are similar and different.

CHAPTER FIVE

The Heart-Centered Lovers: Givers, Stars, and Romantics

Place your heart within my hands and let us see
All the things that our romance was meant to be
Count your blessings, smile and hold me lovingly
Thank your stars that I have you and you have me

Free yourself of spiritless and earthly ties
Hold my hands and let me look into your eyes
Dream with me and our Valhalla will arise
Give me just a little glimpse of paradise"
("Love And," Perman~Clarvit)

Givers

Givers are...well, giving. **Their key Facet of Sexual Expression is Love.**

Givers make themselves available. In other words, they want to be there for their lovers, which moves the center of their sexuality outside themselves, based more on their lover's desires than even their own. This may lead to co-dependency, or can just create a dense matrix of loving acts that some lovers appreciate, while others may feel overwhelmed by, or compelled to take advantage of.

Givers tend to be expressive lovemakers, because the most important thing to them is giving pleasure. They are willing to do what their lover wants, up to a point, and frequently beyond that point. One of the traps of being a Giver is that they will often put up with lovemaking patterns that aren't really satisfying for them, rationalizing that it is part of being a Giver to provide whatever supports their partner's needs and wants, putting their own desires secondary to those external influences.

But if they start to feel underappreciated, then they get needy. And if it goes too far, then they get angry and manipulative. Later, in Chapter Eight, we'll talk more about what happens when a Giver reaches a stress point, so those of you who are Givers can track your feelings and learn how to defuse those feelings before they get toxic.

Like other heart-centered lovers, they tend to lead with their hearts. The form this takes for Givers is in being overtly loving, doting, even smothering at times. They show their love in an obvious emotional fashion. Those feelings make the Giver seem very loving to outside observers, which is exactly how they prefer to be perceived.

Inside, they are trying to make sure they serve the needs of their partner. As long as they get a little something in return, they can keep going with those patterns for quite a while. Givers may feel uncomfortable when this is brought to light, sometimes even evoking denial. They would rather be seen as selfless, since that's the way they prefer to see themselves.

This subtle "give to get" underlies many of the behavioral choices of the Giver, and explains why they may stress if they get to a point where they feel "gived out" because they are not getting what they want and need in return.

Real satisfaction for a Giver is to be given to as well; not because they complain and ask for it, but through their own feelings being supported by their partner noticing and responding. Because they often find it difficult to ask, a Giver's lover needs to intuit or guess, which brings back the crapshoot. So, Givers need to learn how to make it clear how they feel and what they need to be satisfied. They must establish their own identity in the intimate encounter. And a Giver's lover needs to persist in exploring their feelings to uncover what they really want.

The Giver might think,
> *"How can I pleasure you? How can I make myself yours? How can I help you find ecstasy?"*

Givers are willing and partner-oriented. They intend to be of help, service, or support, and as such tend to be flexible and available to do their partner's bidding. But they need to feel acknowledged, and somewhat compensated. If they give too much, too long, or too intensely without a feeling of being rewarded or at least recognized, they will start to get angry, controlling, and even manipulative. It starts with neediness, develops into hurt, and finishes with demanding retribution.

"Hell hath no fury like a woman scorned" was written for Givers who are caught in a stress pattern. But at their best, their giving no longer depends on how they think they're being perceived, and an individuality arises that eliminates co-dependency and helps the Giver see beauty inside, instead of only in the service to others (more about this in Chapter Eight).

Examples of Givers: Richard Simmons, John Travolta, Dr. Ruth Westheimer, Monica Lewinsky, Mother Teresa, Drew Barrymore, Jewish or Italian mothers.

Stars

For Stars, **the key Facet of Sexual Expression is Growth.**

Stars want to be recognized as the center of attention, to have the relationship revolve around them. They want to be regarded as the best at what they do in every aspect of their lives, including relationship.

Because success is so important to Stars, they often dial out of their emotions. They are heart-based lovers who tend to disconnect from their feelings, which they believe could impede or interfere with their movement toward stardom.

Stars tend to be vain, and their appearance is a big part of their power. Even those not blessed with natural good looks will go out of their way to look good, sometimes pursuing alluring makeup and hairstyles or surgical enhancements. The wardrobe of the Star is elaborate, thoughtfully constructed, and classy.

Image is of paramount importance—in fact, generally more important than physical sensations. Again, this is because becoming too engaged with feeling good could distract away from the ultimate objective of being the best, and being perceived as the best at whatever they do.

The way a Star leads with his or her heart is by keeping it out of harm's way, leaving much of their relationship shallow and superficial. This is not necessarily a detriment for them, as it is generally more important to look good than to feel good to a Star.

Because the Star functions more on perceptions than genuine feelings, they can seem distant, or sometimes overcompensate with a form of warmth that is more about how they want to be seen than what they actually experience. They tend to "feel" through others' eyes, and in being the center of attention, may be willing to trade real emotion for the appearance of feeling appropriately, given the circumstances.

The drawbacks of this perspective are obvious. Deep connections would be more difficult to generate, unless the relationship mate is aware of these patterns and can work with them, both to inspire the Star to grow and evolve in the relationship, and also to accommodate the Star by supporting the need for attention and glamour without competition or resentment.

Real satisfaction for a Star is to succeed at the highest possible level and be treated like royalty, while finding ways to generate real connection without a fear of sacrificing the compulsion to be the best at whatever they set their minds to.

The Star might think,

> *"It is, always has been, and always will be about me, even if I skillfully articulate my me-ness to make it seem like it's about you. Mostly I need a lot of attention. I'm high maintenance, but I also want to be the best at everything, including being your lover. I care how I look, and I care how I come across, because my image is all I choose to share with you until I really get to know you."*

Stars can be hostile at times—and self-centered, and self-deceptive—but they can also be driven to improve and be the best. If they can direct their focus to the relationship, they can excel at whatever they decide is important enough—and, what suits their own best interest in the way they are perceived. At their best, they become more connected, more responsible, and gentler.

Examples of Stars: Madonna, Bill Clinton, Sharon Stone, Tom Cruise, Paris Hilton, Michael Jordan, OJ Simpson, Whitney Houston, Justin Bieber, Sting

Romantics

Romantics are very sensitive, self-absorbed, and often see the darker or more tragic side of relationship. **Their key Facet of Sexual Expression is Beauty**.

They are individualistic, unique, and at times, strange. But this grows from a desire to express themselves in their own particular way. They may find themselves in unrequited love, or seek out relationships that are painful or challenging. They do this both to experience the dark side of love, and also to maintain their individuality, opting out of blending with the other and instead retaining the uniqueness of each of the partners.

Romantics are artistic and creative, too, and will tend to explore an inner world of passion that others often cannot connect with or understand. They may have an odd or weird take on intimacy, interpreting their desires and expectations in a novel, personalized way.

Romantics can have a freaky side—their lust for individuality may cause them to choose unusual or provocative sexual practices or fetishes. Their self-absorption may take the form of a fantasy world, or may play out in real life drama of their own design and orchestration.

The Romantic might think,

> *"I am special and unique, and I need special and unique loving. I know I'm different, and while I long for acceptance I enjoy my individuality, and I want to be treated like an individual. Creativity and romance are important to me—but there will be drama and the gamut of emotions as I explore all my feelings; sometimes within a single day, or a single encounter. I'm self-absorbed, and I tend to see the darker, more tragic*

side of things. I may be different, but my differences are important to me and are to be honored."

Romantics may be withdrawn, living a passionate and sometimes bizarre inner life. Or they can overtly act out their artistic flair in melodrama with their family and friends. But they usually appreciate beauty and eroticism, and at their best, harness their creativity into practical and organized efforts, in bed and elsewhere in their lives.

Examples of Romantics: Johnny Depp, Joni Mitchell, Michael Jackson, Sean Penn, Angelina Jolie, Nicholas Cage, Alanis Morisette, The Artist Formerly Known As Prince, Lady Gaga.

Heart-centered lovers are driven by their emotions—Givers by the emotion they feel when serving others' needs, Stars avoiding too much connection so it doesn't interfere with their growth, and Romantics by deep, sensitive feelings and an appreciation for the tragic nature of life.

If your feelings come to the forefront, whether they are feelings of warmth, detachment, or darkness, you are probably a heart-centered lover.

Points to Remember

1. There are three heart-centered lovers – Givers, Stars, and Romantics.

2. Givers show love by serving others' needs. Stars want to be the center of attention and will detach from anything that might interfere with their growth. Romantics feel deeply and appreciate the beauty and drama of relationship.

Actions to Take

1. Imagine you're getting ready for a party, and try on the patterns of Givers, Stars, and Romantics. As a Giver, would you be looking to help your partner get ready? As a Star, would you be preening before the mirror and fishing for compliments? As a Romantic, would you be choosing a personalized and unique style of dress, or considering the futility and tragic nature of party-going?

2. Watch a romantic comedy and look for examples of heart-centered lovers.

A Question to Ponder

Think of someone you know who may be a heart-driven lover.
Notice how his or her emotions seem to support or interfere
with his or her relationships.

Now, let's look at the three types of head-centered lovers.

CHAPTER SIX

The Head-Centered Lovers:
Professors, Thinkers, and Players

In the shadows of the evening I can see your silhouette
It's the vision of you leaving I keep trying to forget
But the dream is there to haunt me thru the hours left unslept
Like the echo of the promises we left unkept

Baby Come Back To Me, Baby Come Back To Me

I remember how I held you but the memory is blurred
By the tears I cannot see through as I think about your words
You said "Love has lost its meaning,
So for me this is the end."
But I just can't help the feeling I want in again

Baby Come Back To Me, Baby Come Back To Me
("Baby Come Back To Me," Perman~Clarvit)

Professors

Professors are knowledgeable, studious, and sometimes arrogant. **The key Facet of Sexual Expression for Professors is Wisdom.**

Professors tend to look at sex as a field of study, curious and interested, and focused on understanding how it all works. They may dive into the technical anatomy, learn unusual techniques and practices, and may become obsessed with a particular aspect of love and/or sex, concentrating their intentions on fully engaging or being thoroughly immersed in that domain.

Professors assume a more intellectual, sometimes distant relationship with sexuality. It's not because they aren't sensitive, but rather because the distance gives them the objectivity to truly understand intellectually what eludes most people trying to comprehend this complicated subject.

The Professor might think,
> *"How does that work? Where do you like to be touched? How hard? How fast? What happens if I do this? How about this? Or this?"*

They enjoy a scientific approach, reading and studying about sex, perhaps becoming expert in an obscure technique or a far-flung sector of sexuality, or even pornography. They tend to love gadgets and gizmos, toys and quirky intellectual sex games, and may cover their great sensitivity, especially when they are first learning about sex, with a guise of being more knowledgeable and experienced than they really are.

When Professors stress, they get arrogant, so their lovers need to know how to respond when this happens. This arrogance is derived from a fear of not knowing, of not being expert in an area they feel they should have mastered. But at their best, they become strong and certain, using their insight to move their attention outward into situations they can lead.

Examples of Professors: Albert Einstein, Kurt Cobain, Trent Reznor, Lily Tomlin, Dennis Miller, John Lennon, Jodie Foster, Stephen King, Agatha Christie, Bill Maher.

Thinkers

Thinkers are competent, effective, and supportive. **Their key Facet of Sexual Expression is Security.**

As head-centered lovers, their support is less about devotion from the heart, like a Giver, and more about responsibility and consistency, based on reason and rational thought.

They may be willing sexually, more because they see it as their logical role, rather than desiring to be fully engaged physically. Since they spend so much time in their thoughts, it may be difficult for them to access the purer, more instinctual physical sensations in the body, though being able to get out of their heads and into their bodies is a sign of sexual wellness for the Thinker.

They may overcerebrate during lovemaking, making them seem preoccupied to their lovers. They are often insecure, wondering if they are performing well or if they are truly attractive. They may fall into the trap of questioning everything they do or their lover does, robbing them even more of a present sexual experience.

This is because they tend to compare the current moment, which is uncertain and unknown until it happens, to past reference experiences about which they have some certainty because they have already happened. Because of this constant desire to compare, it is challenging for the Thinker to be present right now in the moment, and sexual satisfaction usually requires that.

This would obviously make it difficult to stay present in lovemaking, if they are constantly comparing what's going on now to things that have happened in the past, good, bad or indifferent.

Partners of Thinkers must accommodate that, at times, they will not be so enthusiastic or passionate. But their loyalty will usually guide them to let their partner have their way, up to a reasonable point.

Thinkers might speculate,
> "Is this right? Is he/she having a good time? Am I acting nervous? Is he/she losing interest? I think this is fun. It's like when I was eighteen and my friend told me about that hayride; no it wasn't a hayride, it was a bonfire. That must have been hot. I like campfires, roasted marshmallows are yummy, too bad they go right to my hips; do I look fat?"

Thinkers often want the certainty and clarity of a monogamous and dedicated relationship. They see it as an appropriate trade-off to make themselves available sexually, doing their best to be an active participant. On the other hand, because their past references are in such close proximity, they respond badly to being cheated on. While they want to be responsible, violating their code of ethics makes it difficult for them to ever trust again, as the memory usually haunts them.

Overall, though, Thinkers are competent at most of what they do, including lovemaking, especially when they learn how to elude the grip of the past, let go of what was, and be more present in the moment.

Examples of Thinkers: Julia Roberts, Bruce Springsteen, Woody Allen, Diane Keaton, Tom Hanks, Meg Ryan, George Costanza, Jon Stewart, Marilyn Monroe, Ellen DeGeneres.

Players

Players are adventurous, enthusiastic, and fun. **Their key Facet of Sexual Expression is Passion.**

They tend to seek variety, either within the context of a committed relationship, or by pursuing a spectrum of relationships to entertain themselves and keep it fresh.

As such, they tend to be much better at starting relationships than following through on them. This is not because of any inherent disloyalty, but rather because their short attention span makes them wander.

They often have a wild streak, seeking thrills and new experiences. This is driven by their lust for adventure and spontaneity.

The Player tends to think,
> *"If it feels good, I'm gonna do it, as long as there's lots of variety. I like new experiences, spontaneity, and passionate fun. I have a short attention span, so thrill me now, and keep my interest by maintaining a fresh and vibrant, vital attitude and enough newness to change my focus and give me a new look at things."*

Players are capable of longer-term relationships when there is a concerted effort to keep things new and passionate. Often, they have fleeting interests, so their lovers need to stay light on their feet to keep up. They may also have a roving eye; again, more because a shiny object catches their attention than any character flaw. That's why smart lovers of Players keep it exciting and spontaneous, which corrals and directs the Player's imagination.

Examples of Players: Jim Carrey, Cameron Diaz, Robin Williams, Bette Midler, George Clooney, Elizabeth Taylor, Eddie Murphy, Joe Biden, Lois Griffin.

Head-centered lovers use thinking, learning, language, and reference experiences to formulate their sexual realities. Professors have arrogant self-talk, Thinkers have questioning or insecure self-talk, and Players have playful, spontaneous, and adventurous self-talk.

If you find yourself interpreting and experiencing your sexuality through thoughts, you are probably a head-centered lover.

Points to Remember

1. The three head-centered lovers are Professors, Thinkers, and Players.

2. Professors may become specialists or experts in niche areas of sexuality. Thinkers may be insecure and overcerebrating during sex. Players need variety and spontaneity to keep it fresh and interesting.

3. Professors are in their present thoughts, Thinkers are in their past thoughts, and Players are in their future thoughts.

Actions to Take

1. Imagine you are going on a blind date, from the viewpoint of each head-centered lover. As a Thinker, would you be worrying about every detail and getting anxious over what you don't yet know about your date? As a Player, are you looking forward to someone new, and hopefully different from anyone you've ever dated before? As a Professor, are you hoping for someone who will be responsive to your specialized area of taste and expertise?

2. Watch a TV drama, like a cop show or a lawyer show. Pick out examples of Professors, Thinkers, and Players. What do you notice about each type?

Questions to Ponder

Which head-centered lover would be most likely to be fun at a party?

Which would be most afraid of driving in bad weather?

Which would be most likely to prefer a specific fetish or sexual nuance?

Finally, let's look at the three body-centered lovers.

CHAPTER SEVEN

The Body-Centered Lovers:
Dominants, Dreamers, and Elegants

Only got a minute more
Baby make it mine
Hold Me, Hold Me, Hold Me one more time
Woh I know you got to go
Baby change your mind
Hold Me, Hold Me, Hold Me one more time
I don't wanna say goodbye
'Fore the morning light
Hold Me, Hold Me, Hold Me through the night

'Cause honey, when you're squeezin' me
The world just goes away
Leaving now means teasin' me
Baby won't you stay

'Cause when you put your lips on mine
I tremble to the core
Hold Me, Hold Me, just a little more
And when you put your hips on mine
We tumble to the floor
Hold Me, Hold Me, closer than before

'Cause baby, when you're kissin' me
You know you do it right
Don't be gone and missin' me
Hold Me through the night

Baby, you know you get me higher
When I think of touching you, I tingle with desire
First you're making love to me, then you're out the door
I need more, I need more, yes and better than before
("Hold Me," Perman~Clarvit)

Dominants

Dominants are strong, direct, authoritative, and certain. **Their key Facet of Sexual Expression is Strength.**

They will breed confidence in those around them, offering their broad shoulders and leadership in challenging times. They then often create a sense of obligation, based on their need for control.

Dominants may dominate in a relationship, but sometimes they choose very strong partners, which creates jousting for position that usually ends up with negotiated distribution of control. But most often, the Dominant becomes the policy-setter and decision-maker, sometimes attracting more dependent and/ or submissive partners who need them to call the shots, which they gladly will.

Dominants might think,

> *"My rules for you, no rules for me. I need to be in control, and I like to be met with intensity as long as I win. I am compassionate for the weak but I don't respect them, and I don't want to be like them. I can learn to be loving, but first I must feel like you are my equal, and that won't come easy. I may do whatever I want, so hopefully what I want will be consistent with what you want. If not, it will be hard for me to understand why you have a problem with that—it's just me. But once I decide to look out for you, I will do anything to protect you, or at my best, to help you. I enjoy being in control, and I'm accustomed to being the leader, so I don't respond that well to being challenged when I think I should be making the decisions."*

Dominants have their anger close to the surface. In fact, they often think it's normal to express anger, especially when one of their rules has been violated. They may not be angry until something makes them so—when it shows up it is strong, relentless and potentially devastating. So, Dominants have to learn to manage their anger effectively, and lovers of Dominants need to learn ways to defuse the anger, or suffer some consequences.

But at their best, they become loving, service oriented, and kind, and when that is blended with their natural strength, great things can happen.

Examples of Dominants: Frank Sinatra, Roseanne Barr, Russell Crowe, Queen Latifah, Muhammad Ali, Vladimir Putin, Rosie O'Donnell, John Wayne, Courtney Love.

Dreamers

Dreamers are pleasant, self-effacing, and peaceful. **Their key Facet of Sexual Expression is Harmony.**

They are driven by comfort and avoidance of confrontation, so they tend to stay away from conflict. They therefore make easygoing lovers, though their tendency toward addiction may make them persistent and insatiable.

They are self-indulgent, and as such, will succumb to sexual habit, returning to pleasure patterns over and over again like a lab animal orgying on self-stimulation. They are also prone to fantasy, and may even play their desires in their mind. They feel much of the pleasure they would feel from actually pursuing the encounter and not bother, since the extra pleasure might not be worth the risk and discomfort of doing it in reality.

Dreamers love to dream, and may allow a blending of their imagination with their true experience, occasionally blurring the lines. So, the lover of a Dreamer needs to be aware that they may space out or invest only a portion of their outward attention, preferring to float around inside their heads.

But it is not so much a mental process as an instinctual one, one that is centered in the body and in the "gut feel." So, Dreamers often function on auto-pilot, feeling somewhat numb, but seeking physical sensations to feed their desires.

Dreamers generally make good company, as they rarely cause active disagreement. But they may act passive-aggressively, not venting their anger in an overt way, but finding hidden or obscure ways to express their dissatisfaction.

Dreamers may think,

> "This is the way it's always been done, there's nothing wrong or uncomfortable about it, so why change it? I like my physical contact, and regular, frequent sex is what I want. I don't need gourmet, it just has to be comfortable and end with predictable ecstasy. I can accept a lesser standard, and get used to pretty much anything, but I want it to be what I want it to be. And while I may change my habits and patterns over time, my habits and patterns are what I want."

Dreamers spend much of their time floating around inside their heads, imagining comfortable, pleasurable scenarios and living in that lovely internal world. They rarely show anger overtly, but rather squash it down beneath the surface so they don't feel it—but then they may explode over some completely unrelated and often trivial reason, usually in a relatively safe place. After the volcanic eruption there is often damage, but once they get it out of their system, they're okay for a while and go back to their pleasant self, until the next time they boil over.

Dreamers tend to be non-confrontational and numb. At their worst, they are insecure, immobilized by indecision, and weak. But at their best, they can be transcendent—effective and competent in a pleasant and slightly ethereal way, soothing you and partnering with you in seeking heights of ecstasy.

Examples of Dreamers: Barack Obama, Lisa Kudrow, Ringo Starr, Whoopi Goldberg, Ronald Reagan, Janet Jackson, Dalai Lama, Marge Simpson.

Elegants

Elegants are classy, perfectionistic, and rigid in their rules and perspectives. **Their key Facet of Sexual Expression is Fidelity.**

They are well-put-together, neat, and stylish in a proper way. They may have traditional viewpoints on sex and sexuality, even old-fashioned, because they will usually default to what they believe to be the most consistent behavior with their model of sexual perfection.

This frequently takes the form of a more inflexible sexuality. Elegants have rules that feel divinely inspired, rather than personal, so they are intense in maintaining their standards. So, they may be offended by deviations from their image of the norm, and may vilify or ban anything they feel is outside their boundaries.

Elegants might think,
> *"I am particular, and well I should be, it's the right thing to do. I like it orderly, and while I do enjoy a good time, it has to be along guidelines that stay within my integrity and rules structure. I may seem rigid, but I have good reason for what I believe; a reason that's bigger than all of us."*

Elegants can be stiff, both physically and emotionally. Lovers of Elegants will need to be prepared to yield or at least compromise in areas in which the Elegant has strong conviction. When the Elegant moves toward sexual wellness, there is some relaxation, even playfulness. So if you are yourself or are in a relationship with an Elegant, there is more likelihood of exploring new territory when both partners are getting healthier.

When Elegants stress, they start to get melancholy and self-absorbed. But at their best, they are smooth, distinguished, suave, and cultured. They care about the details, being compelled to get things as right as possible, in bed as well as throughout their lives. As they evolve, their faith makes them more adventurous, curious, and passionate.

Examples of Elegants: Hillary Clinton, Martha Stewart, Gandhi, Al Gore, Felix Unger, Jane Fonda, Mr. Spock.

Body-centered lovers define their sexuality through their physical selves—their skin, their genitalia, their hair, their embrace. Dominants are strong and directive. Dreamers are spacy and self-indulgent, and Elegants are proper and restrained. But all lead with their bodies in engaging the sexual encounter.

If you experience your sexuality through your body, whether it's to control your and your partner's physical sensations, to lose yourself in the dream of your sensations, or to carefully monitor and allow only certain sensations, you are probably a body-centered Lover.

Being sensitized to these sexual personality types will give you a sense of identity, as you begin to realize that your own sexual preferences develop out of a particular worldview. This also explains why two people talking about sex often feel like they're speaking different languages—because in essence, they are. Each of these Nine Types has a specific set of filters and lenses they look through, seeing things their way, and that is both the reason for so many sexual problems, and the clue as to the best way to solve them.

Points to Remember

1. The three body-centered lovers are Dominants, Dreamers and Elegants.

2. Dominants are strong and controlling. Dreamers seem cooperative but tend to be stubborn, spacy and habitual. Elegants are particular and perfectionistic.

Actions to Take

1. Imagine you are preparing to go on a date with your partner. As a Dominant, do you want your date to wear a certain favorite outfit, but are you unresponsive to similar input about your appearance? As a Dreamer, are you secretly dreading going, but won't confront your partner who really wants to go? As an Elegant, are you concerned that the seats will be dirty and smelly, and whether or not you need something to sit on to protect your clothes?

2. Watch a game or sporting event on TV. Pick out athletes and broadcasters who seem like the Body-Centered types. What do you notice about the posture of each of the three types?

Questions to Ponder

Which type is most likely to express passion?

Which type is most likely to repress passion?

Which type is most likely to suppress passion?

In the next chapter, we'll look at each type; first, the way they typically show up as average versions of themselves, and then what they look like when they are stressed and unhealthy compared to what they look like when they are functioning healthfully and moving toward sexual wellness. By comprehending these **Degrees of Sexual Wellness**, you can spot where you and your partner are in this sexual wellness continuum, and take strides to move in a productive, positive direction together.

CHAPTER EIGHT

Degrees of Sexual Wellness:
Integration/Disintegration patterns

"Are you saying that once you know your type, you can predict how you're going to behave when you're healthy and unhealthy?"

"Yes, Rebecca, that's right," Doc Rogers responded. "As you move along the Sexual Wellness Line, you act out consistent patterns, which means two things. First, it means you can tell when you are stressing sexually, and second, it means you can move yourself toward patterns of health at will. You can deliberately grow sexually by adopting certain habits unique to your type. And, it's fun and fulfilling, the way great sex should be."

As you begin to notice some of the patterns being described here in your own life and in those around you, you will get more comfortable and familiar with these new ideas. Before long, you'll start to see yourself clearly among these patterns. For now, let's look a little closer at each type, and see what happens as each one moves along the Sexual Wellness Line, from sick to not sick to healthy to well.

Every type has typical behaviors and habits, and those patterns will vary based on the level of health the individual expresses. Let's examine these trends and gain a deeper insight into the nine types.

Talking about sexual personality types makes it seem like someone always shows up the same way, but this isn't so. Depending on the stresses (or lack thereof) in someone's life, and especially the way that individual deals with the stresses, there are numerous gradations within each personality type. Each type will have habits and behaviors that are demonstrated when they are healthy, others when they are average, and still others when they are unhealthy. Identifying these patterns can help you recognize your type, and also move you in a healthy direction once you know your type.

As you remember the sick-not sick-healthy-well line, realize that you are somewhere on that line at all times, in each aspect of your wellness, including sexual wellness. By noticing unhealthy and average patterns and raising your standards so you show up healthy more of the time, and sometimes very healthy, you will integrate the habits of sexual wellness and spend more or most of your time there.

Now, let's look at the Nine Types of Lovers and evaluate the healthy, average, and unhealthy patterns of each.

The Giver

When healthy, Givers are nurturing, kind, loving and supportive. But when they start to stress, they become needy and possessive, doting on those around them to maintain control and keep them around to reciprocate. This happens because the stressed Giver feels like he or she has been giving without being appreciated. If the Giver gets stressed enough, he or she starts to resemble a stressed Dominant—anger and manipulation will start to appear, and the need for control will be turned up. This can produce stalker behavior, as the need for co-dependency becomes pathological.

But when the Giver notices him or herself in an unhealthy or average place, it just takes a reconnection with giving to disengage the unpleasant emotions and re-engage the positive ones.

From a healthy place, the Giver seeks wellness by becoming more like a Romantic—still fully immersed in love, but evolving a self-sufficiency that doesn't require anyone or anything. Co-dependency yields to a loving form of individuality, and beauty becomes unconditional, to be seen everywhere, the route to sexual wellness for the evolving Giver.

The Star

When healthy, Stars are conscientious, ambitious, and motivated to be the best. But when they start to stress, they become hostile and self-deceptive, like misguided royalty, acting like bratty princes or princesses. This happens because the stressed Star loses touch with the value of his or her intended achievement, and gets too wrapped up in the way he or she is being perceived. Winning and looking good become more important than doing the right thing, and in their intensity to come out on top, they are capable of ethical lapses, deceit, blame, and bitchiness. If they get stressed enough, they start to resemble stressed Dreamers—they will begin to shut down and go into a non-confrontational, fantasy-driven internal world where they can maintain their great self-image, even if their actual reality differs.

But when the Star notices him or herself in an unhealthy or average place, it just takes a reconnection with driving toward a worthy objective to disengage the unpleasant emotions and re-engage the positive ones.

From a healthy place, the Star seeks wellness by becoming more like a Thinker—they are still fully immersed in caring about their image, but they begin to develop thoughtfulness, responsibility, and more connection with their own emotions and in relationship. Narcissism yields to a driven form of loyalty and practical integrity; still competent and determined to succeed, but less about me and more about we, the route to sexual wellness for the evolving Star.

The Romantic

When healthy, Romantics are creative, sensitive, and emotional. But when they start to stress, they become dark, withdrawn, and self-absorbed, appearing weird or odd to others. This happens because the stressed Romantic feels like he or she has been misunderstood or judged unfairly, which generates artistic and creative energy for them to invest in some kind of self-expression. If the Romantic gets stressed enough, it can manifest as freaky or bizarre behaviors, and they may start to resemble stressed Givers, with a warped, co-dependent need for others to buy into their strangeness for validation and support.

But when the Romantic notices him or herself in an unhealthy or average place, it just takes a reconnection with individuality and beauty to disengage the unpleasant emotions and re-engage the positive ones.

From a healthy place, the Romantic seeks wellness by becoming more like an Elegant—still fully immersed in beauty and romance, but developing a connection with the world and with higher powers that was previously unavailable through filters of uniqueness and darkness. Melancholy yields to a distinctive form of nobility, fragile and graceful, the route to sexual wellness for the evolving Romantic.

The Professor

When healthy, Professors are wise and knowledgeable in niche areas he or she deems worthy of study and mastery, including unusual sexual tastes or fetishes. But when they start to stress, they become short-tempered and intellectually territorial, wielding knowledge and logic as weapons of cerebral war. Their position becomes a scientific fortress, walling them off behind their argument. This happens because the stressed Professor never wants to appear foolish, especially in something they feel expert in, or feel they *should* be expert in. If the Professor gets stressed enough, they get oppressively arrogant and snotty, and at their worst, they start to resemble stressed Players, scattered and erratic.

But when the Professor notices him or herself in an unhealthy or average place, it just takes a reconnection with knowledge to disengage the unpleasant emotions and re-engage the positive ones.

From a healthy place, the Professor seeks wellness by becoming more like a Dominant—still fully immersed in wisdom, but developing a sense of certainty that allows him or her to emerge from behind the shield of information to really experience the present moment. Arrogance yields to a knowing form of power, and wisdom becomes strength as the energy field grows and is applied to increase influence, the route to sexual wellness for the evolving Professor.

The Thinker

When healthy, Thinkers are responsible and detail-oriented. But when they start to stress, they become insecure, questioning themselves on every decision, leading to paralyzing doubt. This happens because the stressed Thinker is trying to filter the current moment through past references. In their quest for certainty, Thinkers thoroughly analyze stored memories, which they are certain about since they already happened, and compare their present experience to that for interpretation. This makes it hard for Thinkers to get out of their self-talk and into their bodies during lovemaking. If the Thinker gets stressed enough, the insecurity amplifies, and they start to resemble stressed Stars—hostile, blaming, and self-deceptive, with the desire to save face turned up. This can produce paranoid behavior, as the need for security becomes pathological.

But when the Thinker notices him or herself in an unhealthy or average place, it just takes a reconnection with thinking about something to disengage the unpleasant emotions and re-engage the positive ones.

From a healthy place, the Thinker seeks wellness by becoming more like a Dreamer—still fully immersed in responsibility, but developing a more peaceful self-talk where they are more likely to take things in stride and go with the flow, with faith and positive expectancy. Overcerebration yields to a conscious form of inner peace, and security becomes harmony as the questioning slows and self-assuredness grows, the route to sexual wellness for the evolving Thinker.

The Player

When healthy, Players are expressive, exuberant, passionate, and curious. But when they start to stress, they become scattered and flaky, starting things and not following through. This happens because the stressed Player seeks spontaneity and new experiences, but gets bored easily, and so is distractible, bouncing from one fun thing to another. If the Player gets stressed enough, they start to resemble stressed Elegants—nitpickiness and perfectionism will start to appear, and the need for orderliness will be amplified. This can produce obsessive-compulsive (OCD) behaviors, attention to detail gone wild, as the need for variety becomes pathological.

But when the Player notices him or herself in an unhealthy or average place, it just takes a reconnection with enthusiasm to disengage the unpleasant emotions and re-engage the positive ones.

From a healthy place, the Player seeks wellness by becoming more like a Professor—still playful, but developing an inner wisdom that helps the Player discover everything he or she is looking for on the inside, relieving the insatiable compulsion to seek outside stimulation and excitement. Relentless exploration yields to a knowingness with a sense of humor, and playing becomes meaningful, the route to sexual wellness for the evolving Player.

The Dominant

When healthy, Dominants are strong, certain, and assertive. But when they start to stress, they become controlling and manipulative. This happens because the Dominant wants to control his or her environment, for protection, and also getting their way. Turned up too high, anger and power-lust make the Dominant too aggressive. This happens because the stressed Dominant feels like he or she knows best, and others need to listen and respond. If the Dominant gets stressed enough, he or she starts to look more like a Professor—intellectually arrogant and convinced that his or her way is best and others are misguided, or even stupid. This causes a thinner skin, with more conceit and defensiveness, and can produce hater behavior, as the need for utter compliance and obedience becomes pathological.

But when the Dominant notices him or herself in an unhealthy or average place, it just takes a reconnection with certainty and strength to disengage the unpleasant emotions and re-engage the positive ones.

From a healthy place, the Dominant seeks wellness by becoming more like a Giver—still fully immersed in strength and certainty, but developing a lovingness and service orientation that makes a healthy Dominant a great supporter and a committed partner. Control yields to a powerful form of loving support, and opportunities to use power for good are recognized everywhere, the route to sexual wellness for the evolving Dominant.

The Dreamer

When healthy, Dreamers are cooperative, considerate, helpful, and non-confrontational. But when they start to stress, they become withdrawn and aloof, going through the motions and nodding yes to everything, but retreating to an internal world that is more comfortable. This happens because the stressed Dreamer feels like it's easier to dream about pleasure than it is to actually pursue it. In fact, by just dreaming about whatever they want, Dreamers often experience most of the pleasure they would get from actually accomplishing it, de-incentivizing them even more. I mean, why work so hard for that extra ten or twenty percent when they're feeling pretty good already without it?

So, Dreamers frequently underachieve in love; not for lack of talent and ability, but of drive to follow through, both on their inner work and also the shared responsibilities of relationship. And if a Dreamer gets stressed enough, he or she starts to look like a stressed Thinker—overcerebrating and indecisive. This causes even more hesitancy and unwillingness to confront issues and opportunities, defaulting to well understood and well tolerated behaviors only, becoming obsessively habitual and ultimately, terminally dull in relationship, preferring the same patterns over and over.

But when the Dreamer notices him or herself in an unhealthy or average place, it just takes a reconnection with constructive habits to disengage the unpleasant emotions and re-engage the positive ones.

From a healthy place, the Dreamer seeks wellness by becoming more like a Star—still fully immersed in dreaming and optimism, but developing a willingness to engage and drive toward success, to stand on his or her own laurels and be proud of being perceived instead of flying below the radar. Submissiveness yields to a peaceful form of conscientiousness, and it becomes appealing to act rather than stand by and imagine, the route to sexual wellness for the evolving Dreamer.

The Elegant

When healthy, Elegants are smooth, charming, and well-put-together. But when they start to stress, they get stiff and cling to their version of what's right, standing on ceremony and insisting that they are interpreting the rules correctly. Their opinion, therefore, is unchallengeable. This happens because the stressed Elegant rationalizes their prudishness and the ensuing frigidity by blaming it on higher powers and universal truths, absolving them of any ego benefit from the outcomes. If the Elegant gets stressed enough, he or she starts to look like a stressed Romantic—melancholy, self-absorbed, and likely to see the darker, tragic side of the relationship and life itself.

But when the Elegant notices him or herself in an unhealthy or average place, it just takes a reconnection with orderliness and proper rules structure to disengage the unpleasant emotions and re-engage the positive ones.

From a healthy place, the Elegant seeks wellness by becoming more like a Player—still fully immersed in fairness and doing the right thing, but developing a flexibility and passion that generates more fun. Rigidity gives way to a reasonable curiosity, and the stifling rules structure relaxes to permit some adventurousness and fun, the route to sexual wellness for the evolving Elegant.

So, in summary:

> Givers grow to become more like Romantics,
> and stress to look more like Dominants.

> Stars grow to become more like Thinkers,
> and stress to look more like Dreamers.

> Romantics grow to become more like Elegants,
> and stress to look more like Givers.

Professors grow to become more like Dominants,
and stress to look more like Players.

Thinkers grow to become more like Dreamers,
and stress to look more like Stars.

Players grow to become more like Professors,
and stress to become more like Elegants.

Dominants grow to become more like Givers,
and stress to look more like Professors.

Dreamers grow to become more like Stars,
and stress to look more like Thinkers.

Elegants grow to become more like Players,
and stress to look more like Romantics.

These are important clues on how to define sexual wellness for you, and how to get yourself and your partner to **Triple F Squared.** By noticing and overcoming unhealthy behaviors, by observing average behaviors, and understanding how to move toward healthy and ultimately well behaviors, you show up at **Triple F**, your own personal fun-fulfillment formula. By your definition, there is a way for you to feel totally fulfilled sexually, and this formula is the description of those patterns for you.

Identify and refine these patterns, and you can attain **Triple F**. And when your partner does the same, that's **Triple F** times **Triple F**, or **Triple F Squared**, where you and your partner are in full awareness of your own desires, and in full connection with his or hers. With some time invested to evolve this awareness and this connection, you can transform your lovemaking into great sex, because great sex is the outcome of **Triple F Squared**.

Points to Remember

1. Each of the Nine Types of Lovers has unhealthy, average, healthy, and well patterns of sexual behavior. How much time you spend in each area determines your level of sexual wellness.

	HEALTHY	AVERAGE	UNHEALTHY
Type One	The Elegant	The Prude	The Frigid
Type Two	The Giver	The Doter	The Stalker
Type Three	The Star	The Prince(ss)	The Bitch
Type Four	The Romantic	The Oddball	The Freak
Type Five	The Professor	The Scientist	The Arrogant
Type Six	The Thinker	The Insecure	The Paranoid
Type Seven	The Player	The Sport	The Flake
Type Eight	The Dominant	The Controller	The Hater
Type Nine	The Dreamer	The Habitual	The Dull

2. Each type resembles another type when in stress, and yet another type when in wellness. These patterns of integration and disintegration are useful to detect levels of sexual wellness, as well as create insight into each of our sexual identities.

Disintegrative Type (stress) ← Type→Integrative Type (wellness)

Romantic ← Elegant → Player

Dominant ← Giver → Romantic

Dreamer ← Star → Thinker

Giver ← Romantic → Elegant

Player ← Professor → Dominant

Star ← Thinker → Dreamer

Elegant ← Player → Professor

Professor ← Dominant → Giver

Thinker ← Dreamer → Star

3. Understanding your level of sexual wellness lights your path toward **Triple F**, and when your partner does the same, it defines the shortest distance to **Triple F Squared**.

Actions to Take

1. From these descriptions of each type, notice what type or types you seem to resemble most. Which are the key patterns you notice of sexual stress? Which are the key patterns you notice in sexual health and wellness? Identify your typical patterns of behavior, and find them in the descriptions detailed above.

2. Pick out a relationship from earlier in your life, and see if you can figure out why it worked or didn't work, based on the patterns each of you demonstrated.

Questions to Ponder

When do you think ideas like these concepts of sexual
wellness should be introduced into people's awareness?
As young adults? When they enter into a relationship?
At the right time during their childhood? On an as-needed basis?

Now that you recognize each type in stress and in health, let's build a foundation to develop more understanding of how these types fit together by tracing **the origins of the Nine Types of Lovers**. In the next chapter, we'll discover some of the roots of this material, and see how the history of it makes it that much more relevant in this current application. Fasten your seatbelt and get ready to study **The Enneagram of Sexuality.**

CHAPTER NINE

The Enneagram of Sexuality:
The Derivation of
the Nine Types of Lovers

Givers are loving, supportive and kind
Stars need to look like the best all of the time
Romantics are sensitive, self absorbed, tragic
Professors prefer understanding the magic
Thinkers are insecure, questioning all
Players love newness and having a ball
Dominants claim their control with their strength
Dreamers can fantasize to any length
Elegants like when we follow the rules
Nine Types of Lovers, which one are you?

You may be wondering at this point where these distinctions came from. There is a fascinating field of study, riding the interface between psychology and spirituality, known as the Enneagram. This odd word actually refers to a nine-pointed diagram that dates back hundreds of years, which has been used effectively in counseling, business, personal growth, and interpersonal relations.

The Enneagram ("ennea" means nine and "gram" means diagram) gives us a perspective on why we choose the various behaviors we choose. Some relate more to the psychological applications, using the work for therapy and emotional wellness, while others view it as a pathway to spiritual enlightenment. Both are available through this new focus on sexuality, as both your mind and spirit will clearly be nourished by better sex.

The easiest way to begin to understand the Enneagram is revealed through the distinctions of legendary psychoanalyst Karen Horney, who said that people tend to follow one of three basic personality styles. They may be more assertive, more compliant, or more withdrawn.

Within each of these three styles, some will be driven by fear, some by anger, and some by image, or the way they are perceived. These three subdivisions give rise to the nine Enneagram types, and can be understood by the Personality Grid, the chart in Figure 1.

Personality Grid

	ASSERTIVE	**COMPLIANT**	**WITHDRAWN**
Fear	Assertive Fear (7)	Compliant Fear (6)	Withdrawn Fear (5)
Anger	Assertive Anger (8)	Compliant Anger (1)	Withdrawn Anger (9)
Image	Assertive Image (3)	Compliant Image (2)	Withdrawn Image (4)

(Figure 1)

There have been thousands of pages devoted to the colorful interpretation of these ideas, by dozens of philosophers and teachers throughout history. Each type has slang names associated with it, depending on the particular thought leader one follows. In essence, though, these nine types are the foundation of the **Nine Types of Lovers**.

If you want to study more about the classical Enneagram, read *The Wisdom of the Enneagram* by Don Richard Riso and Russ Hudson, and *The Enneagram in Love and Work* by Helen Palmer. These are two quite different interpretations of this highly relevant and useful field of study, and will give you a glimpse into the depth of value that can be gleaned in other aspects of life.

For our purposes, the reason this is important is because it helps us comprehend the basic patterns of behavior of each type. For example, the "Image-driven" types tend to be heart or feeling centered, the "fear-driven" types tend to be head or thinking centered, and the "anger-driven" types tend to be more instinctual or body-centered (some call it belly-centered or gut-centered.)

So:

The Giver, consistent with Type Two in classical Enneagram terminology, is heart-centered and compliant. In other words, they are driven by their feelings, and that makes them want to comply with their relationship mate's wishes and desires.

The Star, consistent with Type Three in classical Enneagram terminology, is heart-centered and assertive, which explains why they are less likely to allow someone else to manage their feelings, so they don't lose the opportunity to remain the center of attention.

The Romantic, consistent with Type Four in classical Enneagram terminology, is heart-centered and withdrawn, so his or her feelings are internal, making them self-sufficient by insulating themselves in an individualized, special, and unique world of their own, which may be tinged with sadness, darkness, or a flair for the dramatic.

The Professor, consistent with Type Five in classical Enneagram terminology, is head-centered and withdrawn, which explains why they have a more intellectual relationship with sex, looking at the science and technology of sex as much as the actual performance.

The Thinker, consistent with Type Six in classical Enneagram terminology, is head-centered and compliant, which causes them to filter their relationship through their thought processes, leading to the potential for insecurity, overcerebration, and doubt, while striving for competence and effectiveness.

The Player, consistent with Type Seven in classical Enneagram terminology, is head-centered and assertive, so they deal with their fears not by analyzing, but by staying in constant forward motion, putting pressure on longer-term relationships which may become boring or unexciting.

The Dominant, consistent with Type Eight in classical Enneagram terminology, is body-centered and assertive, so that they tend to have big energy fields and exert their will to maintain control, believing "my rules for you, no rules for me."

The Dreamer, consistent with Type Nine in classical Enneagram terminology, is body-centered and withdrawn, so they process their reality through internal physical sensations, making them vulnerable to addictions and habitual behaviors.

The Elegant, consistent with Type One in classical Enneagram terminology, is body-centered and compliant, taking the form of righteousness and integrity in their relationships, but with more rigid rules structures about what is permissible physically.

These brief descriptions are not meant to make you an expert in the classical Enneagram material, but rather to serve as a resource to guide those who are interested in further investigation.

One of the most compelling reasons to study the Enneagram is that it provides pathways of growth, not only details about one's current personality expression. Let's dig a little deeper into the actual Enneagram material so you can begin to visualize the way each type evolves in the context of their own sexuality.

Here is a chart that summarizes the nine types, and some basic qualities of each:

Enneagram/Nine Types of Lovers Qualities Chart

TYPE	FACETS OF SEXUAL EXPRESSION	HEALTHY	AVERAGE	UNHEALTHY
One **Elegant**	Fidelity/ Faith / Trust / Honesty	Elegant, chivalrous, grand, immaculate appearance, courteous, excellent dresser, moving toward more expressive fashion and more flexibility and adventurousness while maintaining elegance and natural rightness	Rigid, proper dresser, accurate, reliable, loyal, stuffy, does the right thing, will experiment if it seems safe, clean and right and doesn't take much flexibility	Immobile, inflexible, unwilling, crippled or restricted by narrow interpretation of natural law, puritanical, vigilant
Two **Giver**	Love/Nurture/ Caring	Loving, fully engaged in love, generous, supportive, interdependent, solid, kind	Servile, attentive, giving, slightly begrudging, will do anything for love but must feel appreciated, compensated, in high regard	Needy, manipulative, co-dependent, angry, controlling, resentful
Three **Star**	Growth/ Success	Excellent, devoted to personal growth, seeking advanced levels of ecstasy, seeking excellence in appearance, fitness, wellness, sexual athlete	Vain, self-absorbed, competitive, driven to be the best, disconnected from their emotions, preening, more concerned with appearances than joy, since they don't feel as much as experience what they think they should be feeling	Hostile, cold, vicious, relentless, self-deceptive, self-aggrandizing, narcissistic, nasty, greedy, egotistical, detached, aloof, disengaged, numb
Four **Romantic**	Beauty/ Romance/ Mystery	Romantic, creative, unique, dialed into natural rhythms, artistic, imaginative	Dark, tragic, self-absorbed, odd, dramatic, unusual, individualistic, quirky, artsy, weirdly fun	Macabre, sinister, kinky, fantasy freak, role-player, needy to feed the fantasy, difficult to please, brooding

Five **Professor**	Wisdom/ Common Sense	Intelligent, well studied, interesting, specialized, experimental	Arrogant, wise ass, false bravado, scientific, imaginative, curious	Kinky, sarcastic, self-deprecating and insulting, polarity mismatcher, bitter
Six **Thinker**	Security / Responsibility	Loyal, responsible, willing, engaged, will do anything if it seems like their responsibility	Timid, self-conscious, insecure, uncomfortable, game, counter-phobic, conservative	Fearful, self-conscious, insecure, too analytical, paranoid, hostile, self-deflective, blaming
Seven **Player**	Passion/ Joy / Fun	Adventurous, erotic, passionate, fully engaged, flexible, finds pleasure within as well as from outside, playful	Flighty, flaky, short attention span, great starter lousy finisher, spontaneous, enthusiastic, expressive dresser, outgoing, fun	Insatiable, unreliable, squirrelly, self righteous, perfectionistic, nitpicky, critical
Eight **Dominant**	Strength/ Respect	Strong, powerful, dependable, surprised by their own sensitivity in intimacy, becoming more loving and service oriented as they evolve	Dominating, controlling, crowding, insensitive, uncaring, my rules for you/ no rules for me, big energy field	Violently angry, unable to see boundaries, domineering, unreasonable, arrogant
Nine **Dreamer**	Harmony/ Peace	Intuitive, rhythmic, consistent, profoundly connected, committed, marathon lover	Habitual, boring, ritually obsessed, hedonistic, comfort freak, numb, self-effacing, unaware, pleasant, non-confrontational, patient, nice, deliberate, spaced out	Withdrawn, reclusive, hallucinatory, obsessive, repetitive, addictive, paranoid

Each type has a healthy expression, an average expression, and an unhealthy expression, and they are related in a magnificently orchestrated fashion. This is most easily understood through the classical Enneagram diagram, which looks like this:

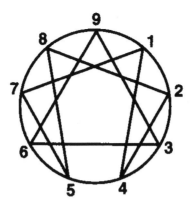

Again, depending on which teachers you follow, there are numerous interpretations. But you can see how the nine types are laid out along the circumference of the circle, and that they are also connected inside the diagram by lines that define the directions of health and unhealthy, integration and disintegration.

For example, look at Type Two, The Giver. When the Giver is expressing typical patterns, their desire to give is so strong they may become co-dependent, needing to be of service to someone to feel good about themselves. That's what compels them to be giving. But look at the inner lines on the diagram—Type Two is connected to Type Eight and Type Four.

Watch how beautifully this fits together. If the Giver (Type Two) stresses, he or she becomes more like a Dominant (Type Eight), since feeling unappreciated makes him or her angry, wishing to seize control so they can feel better. But if the Giver wants to grow, he or she can integrate toward being more like a Romantic (Type Four), and become more self-sufficient and less dependent on others' responses. This separation is very healthy for the Giver, who stops defining him or herself in terms of service to others, and more by his or her own identity.

Here's another example. If the Player (Type Seven) stresses, he or she starts to look more like a stressed Elegant (Type One), overly precise, critical and perfectionistic. But when a player (Type Seven) grows, he or she integrates toward being more like a Professor (Type Five), wise and well-informed, and aware that the excitement and adventure he or she seeks is actually inside, not outside in the form of external experiences.

Another example—when Dominants come out of their baser instincts and move toward their heart center, they becoming more like Givers, unconditionally loving instead of judgmental and controlling. They dissipate anger, relinquish control, and become truly caring, while retaining the power and certainty of the Dominant. This makes them sensitive lovers as well as strong and certain lovers, replacing domination with respect and shared love.

When Dominants stress, their expression of control gets more impatient, arrogant and analytical, like a Professor. So when a Dominant notices these patterns, it's a clue that he or she is under stress, and needs to move in a healthy direction.

And yet another—Dreamers grow by focusing on some target, instead of floating around in the ethers of bliss. They stress by slipping into overcerebration, using thinking and reason where their instincts typically serve them better. In bed, this translates to being present in their bodies, which is why the stressed Dreamer is insecure, hesitant and doubtful. Their mind is not a comfortable place for them to be during lovemaking, as their instinctual sensations and behaviors cannot easily be interpreted through thought.

This system explains why people are the way they are, and how to get unstuck so you can become all you can be. And one of the main places to benefit from this in your life is in your sexual relations. By recognizing which patterns are truly pleasing to you, and which are not, you can move toward your own Fun-Fulfillment Formula—Triple F. And remember, when you and your partner both do this, it leads to the ultimate in great sex, Triple F Squared!

Here's the way each type integrates and goes beyond health to wellness.

Disintegrative Type (stress) ← Type → Integrative Type (wellness)

Romantic (Type Four) ← Elegant (Type One) → Player (Type Seven)

Dominant (Type Eight) ← Giver (Type Two) → Romantic (Type Four)

Dreamer (Type Nine) ← Star (Type Three) → Thinker (Type Six)

Giver (Type Two) ← Romantic (Type Four) → Elegant (Type One)

Player (Type Seven) ← Professor (Type Five) → Dominant (Type Eight)

Star (Type Three)← Thinker (Type Six) → Dreamer (Type Nine)

Elegant (Type One) ← Player (Type Seven) → Professor (Type Five)

Professor (Type Five) ← Dominant (Type Eight) → Giver (Type Two)

Thinker (Type Six) ← Dreamer (Type Nine) → Star (Type Three)

Points to Remember

1. We are all on a gradient between unhealth and wellness, the Sexual Wellness Line™. Using the distinctions in this chapter, you can identify where you are in that continuum.

2. Knowing your type, your integrative and disintegrative types, and the patterns that typically accompany those types, helps us see where we are on this wellness gradient, and willfully move in a constructive direction.

Actions to Take

1. When you are healthy, what patterns do you usually demonstrate? How about when you are stressed?

2. How do these patterns affect your sex life?

Questions to Ponder

What do you think would happen
if people knew about these patterns of sexual wellness
when they were learning about sex?

Now that you understand where these distinctions came from, it's time to learn how they work together, so you can grow and solve whatever problems arise.

CHAPTER TEN:

Growth and Troubleshooting
On Your Own and Together

Baby's on the backburner cooking up slow
She no longer seems to be inspired
And I'm standing with the hose
Wond'ring who put out the fire—or is she just tired
No, baby caught a pickpocket helping himself
Said variety gives life its spice
Now she's toasting his good health
Sipping my tears over ice

It takes two, yeah two
Working together to see things through
It takes two...yeah, two
Isn't it better
With me instead of just you
Oh yeah, it takes two....

Where are the words to say
When love has gone away
Feels like I can't go on trying
Where is the ecstasy
Having you next to me, sighing?
I'm left with memories,
Fanning the flame of desire
And I'm standing with the hose
Wond'ring who put out the fire
("It Takes Two," Perman~Clarvit)

In the preceding pages, you've been exposed to many ideas about relationships, sex, communication, and behavior, and now it's time to develop a specific strategy so you can have great sex. Here are some applications of the systems we've been studying.

Applying the Sexual Wellness Line™

Knowing your type and the type of your partner is like having a window into the inner workings of the relationship. But the basic concepts of sexual wellness and the Relation Equation give you a foundation upon which all great relationships are built. Now that you have some distinctions about the Nine Types, you can see clearly how these basic concepts can be applied.

We can now revisit the Sexual Wellness Line, including the level of health for any type of lover:

Stress type ← (disintegrating) ← Type → (integrating) → Growth Type

Sick ——————————► Not Sick / Healthy ——————————► Well

So, if you are a Giver, for example, then you could find yourself somewhere on this continuum:

Dominant ← (disintegrating) ← Giver → (integrating) → Romantic

Sick——————————► Not Sick / Healthy ——————————► Well

A Star's Sexual Wellness Line would look like this:

Dreamer ← (disintegrating) ← Star → (integrating) → Thinker

Sick——————————► Not Sick / Healthy ——————————► Well

For a Romantic, it looks like this:

Giver ← (disintegrating) ← Romantic → (integrating) → Elegant

Sick —————————→ Not Sick / Healthy —————————→ Well

A Thinker's Line would be represented this way:

Star ← (disintegrating) ← Thinker → (integrating) → Dreamer

Sick —————————→ Not Sick / Healthy —————————→ Well

Here is a Player's Line:

Elegant ← (disintegrating) ← Player → (integrating) → Professor

Sick —————————→ Not Sick / Healthy —————————→ Well

And this would be a Dominant's version:

Professor ← (disintegrating) ← Dominant → (integrating) → Giver

Sick —————————→ Not Sick / Healthy —————————→ Well

This is the Sexual Wellness Line for the Dreamer:

Thinker ← (disintegrating) ← Dreamer → (integrating) → Star

Sick —————————→ Not Sick / Healthy —————————→ Well

And finally, here's the Elegant's Line:

Romantic ← (disintegrating) ← Elegant → (integrating) → Player

Sick —————————→ Not Sick / Healthy —————————→ Well

Locating yourself in this gradient and recognizing the behavior patterns that would move you toward wellness are cornerstones of a great sex life.

Advanced Application of the Relation Equation™

Gaining rapport through matching and mirroring will open the door for powerful communications with your partner about your sex life. Now you have highly relevant and exciting information to exchange, information about your own personal patterns and the patterns of your lover. When you maintain rapport and ask good questions about what you want and don't want in your sexual encounters, you will feel a sense of sexual liberation you've never before experienced.

Staying engaged with your partner through reflecting back their breathing, their facial expressions, their posture, and their voice qualities will generate a connection that will make it feel safe to discuss these very intimate details. As long as you keep rapport, it will be more comfortable to talk about even the most sensitive topics.

If you ask a question that rocks the boat, or is misunderstood, have a safe word or phrase that can quickly get you out of that precarious place. Often, this will happen after some progress was made, and it shouldn't be overlooked that it takes great courage to even begin such a conversation.

You could say, "Hey, let's not go there right now," or something like that, and return to a safer place. You may not be able to get the entire map of your sexuality described in one meeting, though some people do. Rather, look at it as a joyful, entertaining, and thrilling process, where you uncover golden nuggets of sensuality and expand your awareness of your pleasure buttons, individually and as a couple. What could be more fun than that?

Keeping rapport, you can gain permission to ask very personal questions, and to reveal very personal desires. If rapport is broken for any reason, regain it quickly by matching and mirroring, especially breathing. If it gets too sticky, use the safe words to bail out for now, but both take note of the discomfort, because at some point you'll need to revisit it and clear it out. The lure of great sex makes it easier to break through such situations.

Developing an awareness of your type and your partner's type will give you some general guidelines to get started. From there, each person and each couple creates many subtle patterns that make every relationship unique.

Knowing about the Nine Types of Lovers helps you understand the process, saving unnecessary stress and squandered energy, and getting better results faster.

The Nine Types of Lovers Calculator

If you've read this far, you probably have a pretty good idea if you are head-centered, heart-centered, or body-centered, and you may even know which type you are.

But if not, this tool will help you figure it out.

Let's review the qualities of these three basic love styles.

> ***Head-Centered Lover***—*fear-driven, mind full of thoughts,*
> *logic and reason*

> ***Body-Centered Lover***—*anger-driven, going with gut feel,*
> *animal drives*

> ***Heart-Centered Lover***—*image-driven, appearances matter,*
> *emotions rule*

For each of these three basic love styles, leading with the head, heart, or body, there are three types; one more assertive, one more compliant, and the third more withdrawn. Here's how these words are defined:

> ***Assertive Lover***—*strong, dominant, passionate, loud,*
> *aggressive, intense, playful, incendiary,*
> *directive, driven*

> ***Compliant Lover***—*relationship-oriented, supportive, loving,*
> *civil, reasonable, ethical*

> ***Withdrawn Lover*** – *internal, quiet, artistic, creative,*
> *scientific, sensitive, aloof*

Here are six paragraphs, two groups of three, one for each of these subcategories. Pick one from each group that you feel best describes you.

Assertive Lover. *I know what I like, and you are either that or something else. I may be accused of coming on too strong at times, but it's really just that I feel like I know who I am, and I want to portray that picture of myself, so I attract the right kind of relationship mate. I am forceful at times, intensely playful and adventurous at others, and I want to be perceived a certain way. I may like games of control. I may compete with you at times, or I may just get bored too easily and pursue something new. But my power is in my ability to demonstrate my will through action.*

Compliant Lover. *Being connected through communication and love is most important to me. I am supportive and understanding, but don't respond well to disloyalty or being underappreciated. Relationship reigns supreme for me, and I may put my own needs or wishes aside in favor of the greater good, if I see it that way. I am reasonable, civil, and I desire to work things out amicably, though my ethics may be somewhat inflexible in some areas. I will go out of my way for you.*

Withdrawn Lover. *I need space, and I hope you won't interpret that as being about you. I just need to be apart some of the time, or at least have the chance to be alone with myself, or else I will tend to create opportunities for that. I may seem self-absorbed at times, aloof, or even arrogant, but it is usually to protect my boundaries and assure myself of the down time I require. I'll be back, and I can be very nice, as long as you don't ask me to do or be something outside my self-concept.*

Body-Centered Lover. *I come from my instincts, and gut feel is my strongest measurement. I will act primarily on my inner sense of the situation, and even if it comes across as angry, I will behave consistently with that inner sense. I may use my anger as a weapon, may try to restrain it, or may even suppress it entirely, but it is there on, at or beneath the surface. I may have rules that need to be followed, or I may appear non-confrontational or flexible while seething inside. Support or violation of these apparent or hidden rules structures determines the success of my relationships.*

Head-Centered Lover. *I use thought, reason, and language to convey and understand my desires. This stems from an underlying fear, which may manifest as exhaustive study to avoid not knowing what to do, being uncertain and indecisive about what to do, or being so impetuous and curious that I do too much or too many different things. So, I may be adventurous, or cautious, or defensive, depending on situations, but I always respond through some mental process dependent on logic, past reference experiences, or just a pursuit of feeling good right now. I may be a better starter than finisher, or I may be too timid to start at all, or I may start and find fault and cling to a need to resolve the issue. But all of this stems from thinking, study, or mental expectations to be sought and realized.*

Heart-Centered Lover. *Feelings and emotions dominate my experience, whether I feel love, sadness, or the drive to succeed. I may be in touch with these emotions, or I may decide they get in my way and sublimate them. But I operate from my heart, either the light side, the dark side, or from just outside. I may have more me-motions than we-motions, or I may blend into you devotedly and support you in every way possible, no matter how you treat me. I want to be perceived a certain way, and those feelings move me, though they may move me toward you, toward suffering, or may even move me not to feel them because they are obstructions to my success. I may feel underappreciated, or melancholy, or hostile and cold, but these all stem from frustration in not getting what I want.*

By choosing which paragraphs describe you best, you can get closer to understanding your type. Don't take the result as gospel, but rather use it in the development of your understanding so you can decide which of the Nine Types of Lovers you are, based on a variety of perspectives.

	Assertive	Compliant	Withdrawn
Body-Centered	Dominant (8)	Elegant (1)	Dreamer (9)
Head-Centered	Player (7)	Thinker (6)	Professor (5)
Heart-Centered	Star (3)	Giver (2)	Romantic (4)

Recognizing Patterns of Behavior

We tend to develop and follow patterns of behavior, and when these patterns are typical in certain situations, they can be observed and utilized in the communication between lovers.

For example, some people tend to move toward pleasure, while others will move away from pain. Some know things are true because they learn about them, other because they just have a feeling inside. Some people tend to see the sameness in things, others tend to see the differences.

These are all subtle (and not-so-subtle) distinctions that add to your ability to interpret what behaviors you can expect in yourself and your lover, so you can effectively anticipate both positive responses and also avoid unsupportive or undesirable ones.

Pay attention—not to be critical—but to lovingly and patiently identify the little things that make you, you, and make your lover, your lover. This is virtually a sexual fingerprint that is one of a kind. When you remove the symptoms of an uncertain or unsatisfying sexuality, it's so much easier to address the other challenges we face. And when you have the tools and perspectives to create sexual wellness, the communication crystallizes, the friction eases, the progress accelerates, and over time you mold and shape a formula for a relationship and a love life that is fun and fulfilling—Triple F Squared.

How to Target Your Ideal Lover

For those who do not yet have a relationship, you can use this simple five-step process to create one. You may have an advantage over people who already have a relationship in that you can use the principles you have learned in this book to seek someone who is a good fit with you sexually.

The first step is to identify the kind of person you want to attract. The more clearly you can visualize this person, the more likely you recognize him or her when you have the opportunity. Some believe you actually increase the chances of attracting such a person by the act of visualization. You can decide that for yourself; but either way, describe the kind of person you are looking for in writing, in detail.

The second step is to locate this person where he or she is likely to be found. You want to fish in a fishing hole that has the kind of fish you're fishing for. Third, you want to increase your visibility in such a location, so the likelihood of him or her noticing you and becoming interested in you is enhanced.

Fourth, you want to use your best rapport skills to connect with this person when you meet him or her. When you do connect, you want to use your best questions to elicit his or her values, to determine the fit and find places of commonality if you want to go farther.

Finally, as the relationship gains traction, apply the principles you've learned here to establish his or her sexual personality type, and use the patterns that would be pleasing for your partner, as you train him or her to be aware of and choose the patterns that you find pleasing. The more fully engaged you become and remain, the stronger and more fulfilling the relationship gets.

Building a Better Lover

This exercise guides you through a process. It's designed to help you become the kind of lover who would attract and/or optimize the lovemaking you desire. When you create an identity profile of that lover, you'll notice that you are like that person in some ways, and not like that person in other ways. By concentrating on your weaker areas, the places where you are not yet as highly developed, you can become more like that person, making yourself a better version of you. Therefore, you will get results consistent with the positive changes you make.

1. What kind of lover would you need to be to have the kind of great sex you want to have?

    a. Personal qualities or characteristics

    b. Beliefs or philosophies

    c. Skills or roles

    d. Possible stumbling blocks and reframing

2. Why is it important to you improve the quality of your lovemaking?

    a. Values

    b. Goals/Outcomes

    c. Benefits/Consequences

3. Do you have any reference experiences that illustrate the qualities, characteristics and beliefs in (1)?

    a. Write a recalled or vividly imagined description

    b. Create some method of accessing at will
       (affirmation, visualization, anchoring, etc.)

    c. Rehearse creation of appropriate states
       1. Specific combinations of qualities
       2. Specific imagined scenarios

    d. Begin to use in actual daily practice

4. Decide if there's anything preventing you from connecting (1) with (3). Use (2) for leverage to break through, or identify weaker areas and build resources to overcome.

5. Condition new patterns through repetition. Link pleasure to the progress, and pain to the old pattern.

What did you learn in this exercise? How can you use these distinctions to get the most out of yourself? What kind of relationship would you expect to have, upon building yourself in the ways you have just defined? What's the first step? What standard of change and excellence are you willing to commit to? How will you hold yourself to these standards that you have defined for yourself? What will it mean when you do?

If you are already in a relationship, try on these newfound distinctions in real time, and see what actually happens.

If you are not currently in a relationship, then work on becoming the kind of lover who would attract the kind of lover you prefer.

10 Reasons People Don't Have Great Relationships

In *The Seven Levels of Intimacy*, Matthew Kelly shares some valuable insights about the way relationships develop and function. He offers ten reasons why people fail to create satisfying relationships:

1. They don't establish a common purpose.

2. They don't clearly define what makes a relationship great.

3. They make it a moving target.

4. They make it seem impossible.

5. They don't believe.

6. They never make it an absolute must.

7. They don't follow through.

8. They have no accountability.

9. They give up in the face of major challenges.

10. They never get quality coaching.

This offers a wonderful blueprint for a beautifully functional relationship, poised and ready to have great sex.

1. Establish a common sexual purpose.

2. Clearly define what makes sex great for both of you.

3. Agree on a plan to make your sex great.

4. Make sure your plan is achievable and realistic.

5. Believe that you can regularly have great sex.

6. Make it an absolute must to discover your fun-fulfillment formula, and your partner's.

7. Persevere and follow through until you reach Triple F Squared.

8. Hold yourself and each other accountable to stick to the plan.

9. Don't give up in the face of major challenges.

10. Get quality coaching.

DECIDE and SAVE TIME

Let me share two communication models that will help to shape constructive behaviors and shut down less favorable ones.

The first is called the DECIDE model, used to shape behavior. Let's break apart this word and see what we find.

D ynamic

E xclamation

C onscious

I ntervention

D etermined

E xecution

The DE stands for "Dynamic Exclamation." When you are intent on instituting a behavior pattern, the first step is to boldly declare what you intend to do, and commit to it.

The CI stands for "Conscious Intervention." When you first commit to a new behavior, it is not yet conditioned, and it takes some directed effort to nurture the pattern until it becomes second nature.

Finally, the DE at the end stands for "Determined Execution." This is where you persist in your intention until the pattern is installed as a new habit.

The second model is the SAVE TIME model, used for conflict resolution.

S tate

A ssessment

V alues

E licitation

T ranslation of

I nformation

M eaningful

E xchange

The SA stands for "State Assessment." The first step is to take stock of the situation. Notice the state you are in and the state your partner is in, and the conditions surrounding the scenario. Once you see the state your partner is in, you can match and mirror to gain and maintain rapport.

The VE stands for "Values Elicitation." Once you have assessed your partner's state and gained rapport, you must now find out what the problem is, and what's behind the problem. Ask questions like, "Why is this important to you?" so you can identify the rules, values, or standards that are being violated. As you go forward with the process you can either change your position and comply, or reframe your partner's perceptions so you can find some compromise.

The TI stands for "Translation of Information." Here is where you take the data you gleaned from your values elicitation and put it into a form your partner can understand and apply.

And then finally, the ME stands for "Meaningful Exchange," where you and your partner discuss what you have translated, so you can come to agreement on the area of difficulty.

This model will literally SAVE TIME. Having a swift, direct, and effective way to iron out wrinkles reclaims resources that would have otherwise been squandered in inefficient argument and head-banging.

Using the DECIDE Model

Use the DECIDE model to shape behavior.

For example, let's say that your lover prefers that you look in his or her eyes before you kiss. You try to remember, but you keep forgetting. This is a time to use the DECIDE model.

First, make a dynamic exclamation: "I look into my lover's eyes before we kiss!" Say it with passion, with certainty, and with unwavering confidence.

Second, consciously intervene, and keep directing your attention back toward the behavior pattern you want to establish. In this example, be conscious that before you kiss your lover, look into his or her eyes. Use your dynamic exclamation to bring your attention back when necessary.

Finally, hold yourself to the standard of determined execution, and keep running the desired pattern until it is conditioned and happens as a reflex. To complete this sample scenario, you would look into your lover's eyes before kissing, consistently and persistently, until it happens automatically, at which point the new habit is created and the behavior is shaped.

Using the SAVE TIME Model

Use the SAVE TIME model to resolve conflicts.

Let's say that you enjoy oral sex, and your partner does not. This is a common conflict that often sours the sexual atmosphere, either when one partner feels like he or she is not getting the desired experience, or the other feels pressured into doing something he or she doesn't like. This is a time to apply the SAVE TIME model.

Start by assessing the state the other is in. Gain rapport by matching and mirroring, and resist the impulse to stand your ground. This kind of negotiation is more like a dance than a battle. Come into alignment with your breathing, facial expressions, posture, and movement, and you can progress to the next step of eliciting each other's values around oral sex.

Don't settle for crude statements of pleasure or pain, for example, "I just like it," or, "I just don't like it," will not move the process forward. What is it *specifically* that you like or don't like? Do you love the intimacy? The subservience? Does your partner not like the view, the smell, or the taste? Are there subtle hidden meanings to the act that trigger pleasant or unpleasant sensations? It's critical to get this discussion under way, maintaining rapport and being willing to be vulnerable and curious so you can discover the best way to resolve this disconnect.

Once you have elicited the values on both sides, now work toward a translation of information. In other words, make sure you both know exactly how the other feels, so you can strike the right balance.

For example, let's say you discover that your partner just doesn't like the taste and texture of sexual juices, and fears unexpected exposure to them. You could use a condom, dental dam, or piece of clear plastic wrap, which allow much of the sensation but removes the risk of the partner's distraction and non-compliance.

Or, you could discover what's in it for you, and see if there's another way you could get it, perhaps with a different kind of touch using lubricants or other textures that might simulate oral sex. The point is, it's better to face the discomfort of coming to some suitable compromise than to let the disconnection linger and start to affect other things.

Once you have the values translated into a language both of you can understand and apply, then it's time for a meaningful exchange, to agree on the ground rules and put them into play, allowing for some refinement and adjustment along the way.

This use of the SAVE TIME model doesn't only save time, it saves relationships.

Five Sensing

Five sensing is derived from Disney, who meticulously went over every square inch of their properties every night, to make sure everything was perfect for opening the next morning. They spotlessly cleaned, repainted the buildings, replenished the concessions, and even started the music and the popcorn machines right before opening, even though popcorn didn't sell well at breakfast time. But the smell, aaah, the aroma of fresh popcorn added to the experience of the kids and families that walked down Main Street.

So, Disney teaches to five sense—in other words, when you are evaluating your office or place of business, pay attention to one sense at a time. First, just look, notice, watch, and observe. Next, listen to how it sounds, paying attention only to what you hear. Next, direct your focus to how it feels; the texture of the air, the surfaces you come in contact with. Then, concentrate on what you smell and taste, to complete your investigation of the precise details of the environment.

Now, this can be applied in the lovemaking process as well, to get very precise about your Fun-Fulfillment Formula. Five-sense your lovemaking, first paying attention to what you see, and notice the details—the colors of bedtime apparel or linens, lighting, and bedtime grooming can shape the visual impressions. Then, listen—breathing, murmurs, the sound of skin on bedding, maybe some music might be nice, listen, listen, listen. Then feel, just feel, the feelings of your body against his or hers, the coolness of the sheets, the softness of the blanket, squeezing and hugging and stroking and playing. Then, just taste and smell; her lips, his skin, the scent of love, the taste of each other. Five-sensing is really sexy—try it and see.

A Sexual Communication Tip

It's good to discuss your patterns and practices before you embark on any particular sexual adventure, but sometimes you need to course-correct and refine on the fly. This can be a moving target, so here's a fun technique you can use to adjust your lovemaking while in the moment.

Let's say you are kissing your lover's body, and you want to tune your level of intensity to your lover's desire at that instant. It may be awkward to ask "Is that how you like it?" while you are already in motion, so try putting your fingers up to or into your lover's mouth, and have your lover determine the intensity by mouthing your fingers with the desired gentleness, firmness or tempo. It's a delightful and effective way to get sexual feedback, and avoids inelegant languaging, putting up with an undesired sexual texture, or missing an opportunity to pursue mutual ecstasy.

Performance Anxiety, ED Ads and Letting Go

(Your ass is perfect, your breasts are just right, more than a handful is a waste, you look fine in those pants.)

(Thank you for coming so quickly, it makes me feel so hot and irresistible, I love and appreciate the size and shape of your penis, I can do things with it I couldn't do with an oversized model.)

As we grow in sexual self-esteem, the pressure to be like movie actors or porn stars will fade into a sense of natural rightness that comes along with sexual wellness. There may be, however, situations that occur which invite self-flagellation, or at least judgment and self-deprecation. Insecurity about our appearance, since few of us can measure up to what we see in the media, performance anxiety that leads to premature ejaculation or temporary impotence in men, and inability to climax in women is too common. The tools and techniques in this chapter can be applied to counteract, avoid, and eventually obliterate all but the most severe cases.

The drug companies are not dumb. They can clearly see the need to capitalize on people's sexual confusion and frustration, manufacturing and selling pharmaceuticals to force the body's gears when an inner resolution would be so much better when possible. It will be interesting to see how this technology affects people's need for sexual performance-enhancing drugs. In a world where people know their directions to ecstasy, the need for such medical intervention would be restricted to those who have a legitimate physical problem.

And let's go on record right here as saying this—being sexually healthy or well does not mean you will never have less-than-ideal sexual experiences, and having sexual symptoms does not mean you are not moving toward sexual health and wellness. Disengage the sexual behaviors at any given snapshot in time and frame them as part of a longer, broader, more all-inclusive continuum, to better evaluate where you are on the Sexual Wellness Line.

The root cause of the great majority of such suffering stems from misinterpretation about the real guidelines of well sexuality. The moment someone dials into this healthier sexual worldview, the more likely that the sexual environment with produce a constructive, healing, and constantly evolving experience.

Addressing Mismatched Libidos

Even within the boundaries of sexual wellness there is wide variation about frequency, duration, and intensity of lovemaking. Therefore, there is a likelihood that at least some of the time, sexual urges will vacillate, and libidos may be mismatched temporarily. This is the time to use the Relation Equation to keep rapport and elicit values, so the communication is clear. It's also a time to invoke the SAVE TIME model, to resolve the conflicts that may arise as a result of fluctuating or unequal desire.

The tools presented throughout this book can be adapted, and any two people who are determined to have sexual wellness can do it by getting together on the appropriate patterns of arousal, desire, and fulfillment.

I once heard Neale Donald Walsch, author of the *Conversations With God* series, paraphrase Jean Houston, one of the grandmothers of the human potentials movement. He suggested that our weaknesses are often our strengths turned up a bit too high. This can surely be true in lovemaking, where our enthusiasm drives our sexual barometers out of balance. But that also means they can be rebalanced, and these techniques are the best way to do it.

Have a Sense of Humor

Two fleas want to escape the cold weather, and they meet in Florida. One is relaxed, tanned, and happy, while the other one is shivering, beaten up, and suffering.

The relaxed one asked, "What happened to you?" The shivering one said, "Well, I wanted to get to Florida, so I hitched a ride in the beard of a biker, and it was freezing cold all the way down here."

The happy flea laughed and said, "You need to try this; I go to a beauty parlor, and wait for one of the women to say she's going to Florida. Then I fly up her dress and hide in her pubic hair."

The next year, they met again in Florida, and again, the one is relaxed and happy, and the other is shivering. The first asked, "What happened to you?" The frozen flea said, "Well I did what you told me—I went to a beauty parlor, found a woman going to Florida, and flew up her dress into her pubic hair. Next thing you know, I'm back in the beard of the biker!"

One of the funniest, sexiest things on the Internet is *Naked News*, which provides timely news stories by beautiful women who slowly disrobe throughout their broadcast, ultimately ending up delivering the news stark naked, completely nude. It's hilariously funny in its incongruity, but also meaningful in breaking down silly boundaries that previously reflected our uptight attitudes toward some of the seemingly more serious aspects of our modern-day culture.

Have a sense of humor. At times, you're going to need one; but you'll always be better off with it than without it.

The Sexually Well Family— Raising Sexually Well Children

As bends the twig, so grows the tree. We are going to have to come to grips with the massive responsibility of raising children into a sexually well world. This means that we must find ways to share distinctions on sexual wellness with our offspring, at the right time in their development to be able to appreciate the distinctions without undue confusion.

It's not the purpose of this book to explore this topic in great detail, but suffice it to say that children who are raised with a healthy sexuality will be more likely to become adults with a healthy sexuality. As our research continues, we will uncover developmental patterns in sexual wellness, and use them as an adjunct to normal, healthy parenting.

Your Sexual Fingerprint

To troubleshoot your own sexuality, remember that there will be two broad categories for you to be aware of. First, consider the general patterns of sexual wellness, like your position on the Sexual Wellness Line™ and your skill at developing the Relation Equation. Then you can look at the subtleties, idiosyncrasies, and traps of each type that guide you toward your Triple F, and help you support your partner in doing the same. By applying the general structure and fine-tuning by type, a level of precision is achieved that must by definition enhance results. It's like a sexual fingerprint, unique to each individual, and a perfect fit because of it.

These guidelines are your directions to ecstasy, your own special individualized recipe. Invest the time and energy in solving these titillating and productive riddles, and the result will be a lifetime of fulfilling relationships, sexual wellness, and great sex.

Points to Remember

1. Wherever you start on the Sexual Wellness Line™, you can have better sex, and before too long, you can have great sex.

2. There are many tools and techniques you can use to move yourself toward sexual wellness. Become comfortable with the inner workings of the Relation Equation, and apply the principles to keep yourself present and engaged in the lovemaking process.

3. Be certain about your type, and learn the patterns of health and unhealth so you can reset when necessary and preserve the overall forward movement toward wellness.

4. Use the DECIDE and SAVE TIME models, five-sensing, and other approaches to refine your lovemaking process, sanding off unwanted

rough edges and causing yourself and your lover to move toward wellness, fulfillment and ecstasy.

Actions to Take

1. Draw your own Sexual Wellness Line™, and see where in the gradient you are most of the time. How about at your best?

2. Sort through the places where your love life is healthy, and where it needs attention, and identify key intervention points. Commit to a plan of self-assessment, self-adjustment, and self-development.

Questions to Ponder

What would you have to change to
spend more time integrating toward sexual wellness?

How would you help your partner to
move toward sexual wellness?

If you don't currently have a partner,
what patterns would you look for that would
enhance your sexual wellness?

And so, it's time to collect our thoughts, feelings, and instincts on this grand body of knowledge, and put all the pieces together so **You Can Have Great Sex!**

CHAPTER ELEVEN:

You Can Have Great Sex

Ooh baby, you're making me weak
And you're probably the reason I'm losing sleep
It's becoming intense, stopped making sense
It's getting out of hand

Ooh baby I don't want you to stop
'Cause you got what it takes to get me hot
I get lost in your heat, knocked off my feet
I wanna be your man

So watch out, better run for cover
I'm prepared to die
I'm your Kamikaze Lover baby
Too late, no time to recover
I've begun my dive
I'm your Kamikaze Lover baby yeah.

Ooh baby I'm about to explode
Hey, I can't hold back, I'm losing control
It's a suicidal mission, a fatal decision
I just don't understand

So watch out, better run for cover
I'm prepared to die
I'm your Kamikaze Lover baby
Too late, no time to recover
I've begun my dive
I'm your Kamikaze Lover baby yeah.

I'm addicted, shoot you straight in my veins
Afflicted and I'm going insane
All this passion just ain't helping this boy
I'm crashing, don't know what I'll destroy

Ooh baby, you're making me weak
And you're probably the reason I'm losing sleep
It's becoming intense
Stopped making sense
It's getting out of hand

So watch out, better run for cover
I'm prepared to die
I'm your Kamikaze Lover baby
Too late, haven't you discovered
I've begun my dive
I'm your Kamikaze Lover baby yeah.
("Kamikaze Lover," Perman~Clarvit)

It's time to take everything you've learned about yourself, your partner, and the act of lovemaking, and put it all together with some simple organizing principles that will make this whole system easily accessible to you and your lover.

Let's pull some guidelines from what we've discovered so far.

Great Sex Depends On Sexual Wellness

Wherever you start on the Sexual Wellness Line™, you can move toward sexual wellness, the result of which is great sex. You can have great sex when you are willing to discover and implement the definition of great sex for you, and work toward the exhilaration of great lovemaking as a foundation for a fulfilling relationship.

Move yourself and your relationship toward increased sexual wellness by developing your Relation Equation. Learning to gain and maintain rapport will enhance all communication, but it will skyrocket your sexual communication. When you breathe together, move together, and build your connection into a mature and satisfying resonance, within the context of each lovemaking session and over the long haul, you set the stage to get the most out of your actual lovemaking. And then, when you solve the riddle of your own sexual desires, you find your Fun-Fulfillment Formula, or Triple F. And when your partner does the same, the intersection of that is called Triple F Squared, meaning that both partners are experiencing sexual ecstasy, fulfillment, and wellness.

Foreplay Never Ends

For generations we have been hypnotized into thinking that foreplay starts when you get into bed and start kissing, cuddling, and caressing each other. This is surely a wonderful thing to do. But if your foreplay starts there, you are missing out on one of the fundamental secrets of all those who have great sex— foreplay never ends. It doesn't start when you begin the formal lovemaking process, it starts the moment you finish making love, continues throughout the time you are not making love, and keeps going up until the next time you make love. Foreplay never ends!

It's the gentle squeeze of gratitude and satisfaction when you release your loving embrace after climax. It's the sweet and/or sexy things you say to each other as you drift off to a blissful sleep, with thoughts of your man or woman in your mind and sensations still tingling on your skin.

It's the enthusiastic and genuine "I love you" that starts your day, and the thoughtful way you do nice things for each other. It's the acknowledgment of each other when you connect, when you part, and when you re-connect, whether in person, by phone, online, or whatever.

It's the kind compliments about each other's appearance, about each other's acts of support, about each other's willingness to be there and do for the other. It's the constant positioning of your partner as desirable, appealing, and attractive. Foreplay never ends.

It's the hugs along the way, and the backrub when it's least expected but greatly appreciated. It's the foot massage after a long day on his or her feet, not asked for, but given gladly. It's gaining and maintaining rapport during a necessary but uncomfortable conversation, and the benevolence of making a space for your partner's differing opinion at times. It's never blaming or making the other wrong, but rather realizing that you can disagree on some opinions without making the other undesirable out of proportion to the disagreement.

Foreplay never ends, and before very long, you are going to find yourself in a loving encounter with this person—never, ever, ever forget it. It's one of the magical keys to great sex—everything you do affects your lovemaking. If you have been unpleasant, or unsupportive, or bitchy, or uncooperative, those sentiments will linger. Wouldn't you rather have your finest moments in your lover's mind when you are about to engage sexually? If so, then you can see the logic of creating as many positive, loving, and endearing scenarios as you can. It leaves a residue of appeal, rather than a mixed bag of emotion. Which would you prefer?

Keep it in mind—foreplay never ends.

Know Your Definition and Your Partner's Definition of Pleasure and Pain

Up until now, fifty thousand words into this book, I have resisted the impulse to include lots of personal stories about myself and my lovely wife, Regina, who has made the last forty-three years heaven on earth, and whom I can never repay for all the good she's done for me. She prefers that our own sex life remain private, and because I want to support her values (see the Relation Equation) I have used other examples to illustrate these ideas.

But here is one area I think Regina will have no problem with me revealing, as it demonstrates a common disconnect for many couples, and offers a simple tool to address it.

My beautiful, sexy wife loves to be teased with quick, gentle touches that thrill and excite her. I prefer broad, consistent touching, like rubbing or squeezing. So, because we tend to extrapolate our own definitions to our lovers, she thought I would like some teasing and tickling, which I find irritating and distracting, while

I thought she would appreciate some stroking and rubbing, which she found relaxing but not sexy.

It wasn't until we compared notes that we realized the trap we had fallen into, one almost all lovers need to learn to navigate. Now, I do my best to remember to tease her with feathery, sudden, and gentle touches, and she avoids tickling and teasing me, choosing instead to fondle, grope, and stroke me the way I like it.

Do we get it exactly right every single time? No, and neither will you. But when you are able to see your lovemaking as a continuum, where there are ebbs and flows, swells and releases, then each experience brings something unique, even if it's the opportunity to notice what doesn't work as well as something else. In that way, you continue to refine and master the philosophy, science, and art of great sex. Even after four decades of lovemaking, we are still learning about each other, and enjoying the process.

Could it really be that simple? Simple, yes, but easy, maybe not. Too often, couples fall into the traps of blaming, shutting down, pressure, or looking elsewhere because their efforts to make it work with their partner have been too frustrating. But with the understanding of these foundational sexual wellness principles, and the incredibly precise and potent application of the Nine Types research, amazing healing and amazing peaks of exhilaration are available. If you know your directions to ecstasy, you'll find your way there—and the journey is really, really entertaining.

That's why we need to consider the Sexual Wellness Line™ and the Relation Equation, even before we look at the Nine Types of Lovers. If you are far to the left on the Line, deep into unhealth, you will have to take these ideas and integrate them at your own pace, hopefully with the full support and understanding of your partner, if you have one.

If you are at the Not Sick/Healthy juncture or better, you should have no trouble gaining rapport and asking some questions about the lovemaking experience. Connect, then discover each other's definitions of sexy fun, and practice them in a safe setting. This is very entertaining, once you get past the feeling of it being weird to be doing it in the first place. But handle that, and this will provide a lot of useful distinctions about what feels good and what doesn't. In other words, you'll be solving the riddle of your and your partner's rules for pleasure and pain, the details of Triple F Squared, your most direct route to sexual wellness.

Don't Pick Your Lover by Type, Pick Your Lover by Energy

It seems logical that if you know your type, and you know the types of lovers that would tend to connect best with your type, then you should look for someone of a particular type, right?

Well, no, not exactly.

You may or may not be able to outsmart the fickle finger of fate. You may be destined to spend your life, or at least your sex life, with a particular type of lover, for reasons that transcend our ability to comprehend them. You may find yourself falling in love with the most unlikely fit, and if so, it would be foolhardy, in my estimation, to break up a naturally right relationship because of someone's type. If you understand this material thoroughly enough, you realize that any two people who decide to have a great intimate relationship can, as long as they notice and follow through on the distinctions we've laid out in this book.

Might it be easier with someone who is a great fit? Yes, but it would probably eliminate 89% of your potential lovers to focus in on one type. And anyway, part of the fun is discovering someone's patterns and learning how to work with them to create the relationship you really want. Besides, the dynamic tension that develops between dissimilar polarities generates a greater response potential, more heat and more passion. Depending on your type and your values, this may appeal to you... or not. Either is fine, but if you are dedicated to having great sex, it will lubricate the relationship for both partners to be able to solve the riddle of connection. Clearly, people of different types can have similar values, and this commonality, along with good rapport skills, can lead to a great relationship with great sex, regardless of type.

It's a better strategy to choose someone you feel attracted to and like being around. Select your lover by energy, not by personality type, and you'll have a firmer foundation to build upon.

Learn the Patterns of Your Type and Your Lover's Type

Though it is possible to create a great relationship, with great sex, with any partner who shares your commitment, the entire process is streamlined and facilitated by knowing the patterns of your type and your lover's type. By now, you should have a pretty good idea whether you lead with your head, your heart, or your body, and from there, the determination of type is merely a process of elimination. Try on the patterns of the three types you could be, and see which resonates best. You can also use the Nine Types Calculator found in Chapter Ten to help if necessary.

Identify the patterns of well sexuality for you and your lover, and explore them, experimenting with different sexual practices until you find those that are truly fulfilling. This is the way to Triple F, and to Triple F Squared. It's unlikely you'll ever find any shared experiences that will be more satisfying, uplifting, and enjoyable.

Each type demonstrates some key qualities and habits, and being conscious of these patterns is useful in constructing your awareness of your type and your partner's type. There will be a range or gradient which illustrates the level of sexual wellness; in other words, the location on the Sexual Wellness Line™.

Habits like a willingness to calibrate desire (knowing what pleases you), developing effective boundaries (it's okay to say no if you do it right), setting priorities, grooming, sexual fitness, communication, balancing the six human needs (certainty, variety, significance, connection, growth, and contribution), reducing or eliminating tolerations, definition of relationship, and safe words for subtle redirection are all fair game for shaping the optimal habit configuration.

Key qualities that may be useful could include self-esteem, confidence, passion, motivation, creativity, kindness, honesty, congruency, respect, and love.

Great Sex Comes From You, Not To You

Genuine sexual wellness is an inside-out process. It starts when you take responsibility for your own satisfaction, through self-study and clean communication with your lover about what you discover. If you wait around for your partner to stumble onto your directions to ecstasy, the inefficiency and distraction will usually hinder your progress.

Be willing to explore your own sexual sensations, to find which sexual practices are most fun and fulfilling for you. This kind of experimentation can be entertaining, or it can be intimidating. But unless you decide to identify your own formula, you can't expect someone else to do it. You can't hit a target unless you aim at it, and you can't aim at a target if you don't know what it is.

Great sex is inside-out, not only outside-in. Who you are determines how well what you do in bed works. Once you know your type, it becomes a platform to push up from. You and your partner can use that information to design sexual practices that you both really, really like, and that's what great sex is made of.

When Two People Have Rapport, The More Congruent Prevails

Relationships are not static. They are dynamic, changing, and growing as time passes and intention is invested. When you are connected to your lover, there is a flow of energy and intentionality that manifests, and that energy tends to grow out of authenticity.

Therefore, whoever is more certain of their sexual status will tend to dictate the potency and consistency of lovemaking. This means that whoever is stronger in their sexual identity will define the actual experiences. That's why communication is so critical—the possibility of one partner's desires being swallowed up by the other's looms large in the bedroom.

So, when you gain and maintain rapport, remember to express yourself honestly and definitively, so your sexual intentions are considered fairly in the process of establishing your definition of great sex.

When two people are in relationship, the more congruent prevails. The one with more certainty directs the flow of information and energy. If the direction favors integration, both prosper. If the direction favors disintegration, both wither, or one grows with friction while the other stagnates. Learning these patterns can help you avoid unnecessary pain and establish an environment conducive to loving intimacy and the desired physical rituals of ecstasy.

Nothing Has Any Meaning But The Meaning You Give It

You have probably noticed that there isn't much information in this book on specific sexual practices. Masturbation, pornography, fetishes, LGBTQ, SMBD, fantasy role playing, swinging, toys, and exotic sexual positions and configurations are just a few examples of the myriad permutations and combinations of behaviors that will be considered in future books. But the big frame around great sex is this: some people like vanilla, some like chocolate, and some like peppermint tutti-frutti with colored sprinkles, marshmallows, and almonds. And each of us is surely entitled to our own definition.

What is odd or kinky for one person may be mainstream for another. Ascertaining your Kinkiness Quotient (KQ) and that of your lover is a pursuit that never fails to open doors of possibility. It's essential to have these conversations that uncover values hierarchies, to define the optimal route to sexual wellness for you and your lover.

You may want to calibrate your Kinkiness Quotient by locating yourself on this graph:

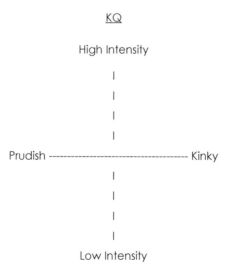

Save your judgment, and instead open up to the discovery of your lover's sexual fingerprint. There is no one else quite like him or her, and together you can assign the most empowering meanings possible to your assorted lovemaking practices.

If You Love Making Love, Making Love Will Love You

Remember, the ultimate outcome of these ideas is to generate a formula for fun and fulfillment, Triple F, and to participate in your lover's unfoldment and evolution of his or her own recipe, leading to the glorious result known as Triple F Squared.

This takes some dedication, some patience, and some tolerance, because it is not often a straight line. Rather it is a convoluted and highly pleasurable journey that meanders through a variety of side excursions and occasional dead ends that necessitate a retracing of steps to get back to common denominators and re-establish a firm footing.

Don't dread this, but embrace it. It's the surest method of creating sexual wellness, and is worth the arduousness of the process. Learn to love this shared evolution, and to honor it, and it will reward you with a lifetime of great sex.

Points to Remember

1. Great sex depends on sexual wellness.

2. Foreplay never ends.

3. Know your definition and your partner's definition of pleasure and pain.

4. Pick your lover by energy, not by type.

5. Learn the patterns.

6. Great sex comes from you, not to you.

7. When two people have rapport, the more congruent prevails.

8. Release judgment and be curious, objective, and playful in sexual discovery—nothing has any meaning except the meaning you give it.

9. If you love making love, making love will love you back.

Actions to Take

1. If you have a lover, read this book again together, making comments and exchanging perspectives to find your commonalities, sticking points, and growing edges.

2. Get certainty about your type and your lover's type, and discover your Triple F and Triple F Squared patterns. Use the Nine Types of Lovers Calculator if you need it to pin down your own type or that of someone you care about.

3. Have great sex!

Questions to Ponder

If there were no rules and I couldn't fail,
what would my sex life be like?

Who would I have to be or become to have this sex life?

By now, you have a grasp of the basis for sexual wellness: the Sexual Wellness Line™, the Relation Equation, and a method for evaluating your type and your degree of health within that type. Now, it's time to take these principles and create the best love life you can possibly experience!

No matter where you are on the Sexual Wellness Line™, no matter how inexperienced you are with relationship skills, and no matter what type you are and how healthy or unhealthy you are in those patterns, there is a way for you to get to sexual satisfaction and sexual wellness. It's based on you discovering your

Fun-Fulfillment Formula, Triple F, and designing your lovemaking by incorporating your partner's definition for sexual satisfaction as well. This leads you to Triple F Squared, the shortest distance to sexual wellness and great sex.

This is a new way of looking at the patterns of sexuality. It cuts across all sexual boundaries, transcending straight and gay, inexperienced and veteran, young and old. It's cross-racial, cross-socioeconomic, cross-faith, and cross-gender. It simply applies to everyone.

It's finally time for us to tackle the responsibility to heal the effects of chronic sexual stress, and launch our society into a new era that is no longer encumbered by the vestiges of our Puritan origins. Our future is bright, lit with the beacon of sexual wellness, which cannot help but rectify so many other challenges that have hindered our evolution.

Now enjoy your pursuit of sexual excellence, and let's build a culture of people who are sexually well, with all the benefits that come along with such a worldview.

And always remember—You Can Have Great Sex!

Ralph and Rebecca were lost in their gaze, breathing in harmony, holding each other lovingly. They had completed Doc Rogers' training, and this was more a celebration of victory than a final exam, following their directions to the ecstasy they both always dreamed was possible but now had discovered how to reveal and share.

They knew their patterns, and were committed to delivering on their promise to each other, following the guidelines they had derived that were theirs alone.

Rebecca trembled as Ralph touched her, melting into his embrace, offering herself to his every desire. She was free, finally free of the shackles of her thoughts, liberated once and for all from the boundaries she once believed she needed, ready to accept him, and accept him she did.

Their eyes locked as he slid against her, aroused and eager to enter the realm of Triple F Squared. In one movement they were joined, rocking together in juicy connection, kissing and fondling and exploring, and passionately feeling everything that could be felt between two people.

Ralph's dream was coming true. Rebecca was his, body, mind and spirit, and his soul leapt with the realization that this was their new reality, the way it would be from now on.

As they bucked and careened, their tongues tangoed, their caresses intensified, the sexual heat built, baked and sizzled, and they knew climax would not be far off. So they slowed their pace, savoring the sensations just as they had planned to prolong the magnificence of the moment, and still squeeze all the pleasure from it.

But love would not be denied, and they erupted, a wet rush of orgasmic delight that only signified how far they had come, and how far they had yet to travel together.

To be continued...

BONUS SECTION:

Encyclopedia of Relationships:
How the Nine Types Love and Are Loved

Now that you have a working knowledge of the Nine Types of Lovers, you can understand how relationships form and are developed. Each type brings something unique and special to the couple (if your definition of great sex revolves around couples; and if not, you can still use this information to assemble any configuration you desire).

Here is the fine detail on combining each type with every other type, a complete definition of each pair of people who could create a loving relationship, and how they can do it best, leading to great sex.

In the back seat of your car
Desperate lovers, that's what we are
Got a feeling over you
And I know that you're feeling it too

I wanna find something in you baby
Don't you know I want inside of you baby, baby
Feeling you hold me tight, hear you sigh
As my hand slowly inches up your thigh
Leaving trust in the dust
I don't care if it's love or it's lust

I wanna die with you, baby baby
See the sparks start to fly with you baby, baby
Making sweet love, making it all night long, pretty baby
Oooh That's why you gotta
Squeeze It To The Last Drop, Baby, Baby

On a lonely one-way street
Desperate lovers lost in the heat
Don't you need me, maybe not
But tonight baby I'm all you got

I wanna burn with you baby baby
Every muscle in me yearns for you baby, baby
Driving me wild, getting me riled for you, pretty baby
Oooh That's why you gotta
Squeeze It To The Last Drop, Baby, Baby

Down on the boulevard and there's no one in sight
I wanna love you so hard
Don't you tease me, come please me tonight
Come on and Squeeze It To The Last Drop Baby
("Squeeze It To The Last Drop," Perman~Clarvit)

So, before we investigate how to apply all this new information so you can have great sex, let's take stock of where we are in this process.

First, we looked at wellness and related it to sexuality.

Next, we looked at the Relation Equation, so you would have a clear view of what it takes to connect with your partner.

Then, we began to categorize lovers into types; some who lead with their heads, some who lead with their hearts, and some who lead with their bodies. You began to look at your own sexuality as a creative process that starts some-place, goes someplace, and ends someplace.

At the climax of this analysis, we looked at the Nine Types of Lovers, so you were able to get a glimpse into that which makes you, you, sexually. This fingerprint, while following certain patterns, is uniquely you, based on how the various gra-dations and distinctions of each type fit together in your particular personality.

Finally, it's time to explore how each type initiates, maintains, and follows through on their sexuality, the culmination of which is great sex. And it starts by understanding how each type loves and is loved.

Let's look at each type, and see which patterns of fulfillment tend to fit, which tend not to, and how those patterns interact with the patterns of all the other types.

Givers

Givers are driven by their need to be perceived as helpful, supportive, and service-oriented lovers. Therefore, they are likely to go out of their way to make their partners feel happy and loved. Their key Facet of Sexual Expression is Love.

What the Giver Needs

Givers don't like this about themselves, because their self-image is one of selflessness; but the raw truth is that Givers want to feel appreciated. They want acknowledgment, and when they are sexually giving, Givers want to be recognized for it, though they'll deny it at every turn.

If your lover is a Giver, let him or her give to you, but then make sure there is some reward in return, to keep the balance and to avoid the Giver stressing, which would make them needy and ultimately angry and controlling.

How the Giver Sees His/Her Partner

The Giver regards his or her partner as a focus of adulation and worship, to be revered and adored. This takes considerable energy, which is why a Giver will get "gived out" if they don't feel some response based on their giving. It's a delicate balance, as they will deflect overt praise, so if your lover is a Giver, allow him or her to serve you, but find subtle ways to return the compliment.

How the Giver Interacts With the Other Types

Givers are heart-centered types, so the shape of their interaction with other types revolves around their heart space, and the demonstration of their lovingness. In sexuality, this takes the form of a willingness to do whatever their lover deems pleasurable, often at their own expense or comfort. Putting their own needs second is characteristic of the Giver, and it's the reason why partners of

Givers need to be prepared to give back at some level. Let's look at how Givers interact with each of the other types of lovers.

Giver-Giver: The double Giver couple creates an atmosphere of unconditional love and support. Each partner tries to outdo the other, and as long as the level of health is good, these couples develop warmth, mutual appreciation, approval, and overt kindness. In the sexual encounter, Givers look for ways to please the other, so a double Giver couple will have to go through the process of learning how to be given to. Since each defaults to serving the other's needs, there will be a learning curve while they work out the details, but the outcome is usually good. Givers stress toward becoming more like Dominants, so if one starts to get angry or controlling, the other needs to notice and give him or her an opportunity to do something helpful, which will usually spur a positive integrative movement. At their best, double Giver couples grow toward becoming more like Romantics, which diminishes co-dependency and increases self-sufficiency on both of their parts, making the relationship that much healthier and that much more exciting.

If you are a Giver with a Giver partner, you can have great sex when both Givers feel good giving to each other, and also receiving from each other.

Giver-Star: Givers enjoy serving Stars, and Stars love the attention. Stars tend to be wrapped up in themselves, and that makes them a perfect receptacle for all of the Giver's affection and love. The problem is that Stars tend to be less warm, and shut down their emotions to prevent them from interfering with achievement. So Givers with Stars will be tested at times to maintain their lovingness, even when they get back hostility and coldness. The Giver has to watch out not to stress, because Stars respond poorly to being controlled. But at their best, Givers can make Stars feel appreciated, their highest value, which leads to better connection in the sexual encounter.

If you are a Giver with a Star partner, you can have great sex when the Giver gives what the Star needs, and the Star recognizes the Giver for doing so.

Giver-Romantic: Givers integrate by becoming more like Romantics, so a Romantic is a great partner for a Giver, likely to inspire self-sufficiency and reduce co-dependency. It is true, though, that when two people are in rapport, the more congruent prevails, so in Giver-Romantic couples, as with all couples who are in each other's direction of integration or disintegration, the stronger of the two will dictate the flow of relationship energy. Hence, in a Giver-Romantic couple, the Romantic must remain stronger than the Giver to make a healthy space for the Giver to grow into. If the Giver is stronger, the couple begins to resemble a stressed Giver-Giver couple, as the Romantic stresses toward being more like a Giver. But at their best, a Giver-Romantic couple has the potential for both of them to grow in love and self-concept without losing themselves in each other.

If you are a Giver with a Romantic partner, you can have great sex when the Romantic is strong, breaks the patterns of co-dependency, and inspires self-sufficiency in lovemaking, not defined only by the other, but including both as individuals.

Giver-Professor: Givers want to serve, but Professors, as head-centered lovers, are more interested in the mechanics and inner workings of lovemaking than the actual experience of being present in the sexual encounter. So, Givers may find Professors to be more clinical and scientific than they might prefer. They get used to it, as Givers are always looking for ways to be pleasing and helpful, and the Professor has no problem defining that space. Givers learn to satisfy the odd or whimsical desires of the Professor, accommodating the unusual by just clas-sifying it as serving their partner, even when things get weird...which they may with a Professor, likely to explore specific practices he or she finds appealing, but most would not understand. Giver-Professor couples have an odd dynamic in that the Professor grows by becoming more like a Dominant, where the Giver stresses by becoming more like a Dominant. So, when the Professor grows and becomes more certain and controlling, the Giver must really be strong or get pulled into a stress position. But if they maintain their center, the Professor con-tinues to grow, becomes more giving and loving, and those are the best condi-tions for this configuration.

If you are a Giver with a Professor partner, you can have great sex when the Giver acts as a receptive subject in the Professor's research, and the Professor is astute enough to appreciate the Giver for doing so.

Giver-Thinker: Because Thinkers are doubtful by nature, loving service may become a moving target in the Giver-Thinker couple. The Thinker may change his or her mind, or just see things differently based on the current conditions, and the Giver needs to stay light on his or her feet to stay abreast of the newest development. Givers will find Thinkers grateful receivers, so they can lavish the Thinker with love to their heart's content and the Thinker will accept it, though he or she may always have an element of uncertainty, even for no particular reason. When the Thinker stresses, Star behavior comes out, hostile and self-absorbed. But at their best, Thinkers act more like Dreamers, and the Giver will find them avid participants in all aspects of sexuality, especially when being given to.

If you are a Giver with a Thinker partner, you can have great sex when the Giver's lovingness takes the Thinker out of his or her thoughts and into his or her instinctual tendencies to be present and conscious during lovemaking.

Giver-Player: As Players are the most adventurous lovers, Givers have to get their roller skates on to keep up with Players. They will probably test the Giver's flexibility, as their curiosity will tend to push the sexual envelope. Givers will, by nature, intend to be there in whatever ways the Player desires, and that may create friction when the Player's needs fall outside the Giver's boundaries. If the Giver stresses toward being more like a Dominant, there will be some head-butting, since the Player wants to play and the Dominant want to control. But when the environment is supportive of the Player integrating, they learn to find passion inside themselves like a Professor; not just in their adventures, and this makes it much easier for the Giver to give appropriately.

If you are a Giver with a Player partner, you can have great sex when the sexual generosity of the Giver is channeled into the fun and playful worldview of the Player, and the Player acknowledges the willingness and spontaneity.

Giver-Dominant: As you've seen throughout this section, Givers stress toward being more like a Dominant, so Giver-Dominant couples have tremendous potential for growth, and also for pain. If the Giver is stronger, and the Dominant is inspired to be more loving, the partnership works famously. If the Dominant is stronger, and the Giver stresses toward being more like a Dominant, it resembles two Dominant types jockeying for control, power, and position, and giving is supplanted by battling. When this happens, it's usually up to the Giver to notice, and to restore a giving atmosphere, so the Dominant has a place to grow into.

If you are a Giver with a Dominant partner, you can have great sex when the Giver is the stronger of the two, inspiring the Dominant to moderate their control and grow toward being more like a Giver. This is where the relationship starts to resemble a double Giver couple, making the overall conditions less controlling and more loving.

Giver-Dreamer: The Dreamer absorbs mass quantities of service, feeding his or her fantasies and inner worldview, so the Giver will find the Dreamer easy to please and cooperative. The problem is, the Dreamer becomes complacent and may forget to give back, or even to acknowledge the giving, which tends to anger and stress the Giver over time. This stresses the Dreamer toward being more like a Thinker, insecure and overcerebrating, and the anxiety triggers in the Giver a deeper need to give, but not from a sexually exciting place, but rather a helping, service-oriented place, which is not especially arousing. This "parenting" pattern may be counter-productive to the development of the adult relationship, though some certainly seek out this parental replacement and enjoy it as part of their sexual practice, like for example in a May-December relationship where one partner is much older, or in role-playing and fantasy play like diapering, dressing like school children, or nursing.

If you are a Giver with a Dreamer partner, you can have great sex when the Dreamer identifies the way he or she would like to be made love to, and the Giver offers that or something like it. The Dreamer must remember or be reminded to acknowledge the Giver, as Dreamers can be spaced out and disengaged in situations like that.

Giver-Elegant: Elegants need the rules followed, so Givers will need to serve their Elegant partners with precision and certainty. Elegants require a well-defined propriety, which will cause the Giver to shift his or her needs to fit those of the Elegant. In the absence of that, the Elegant stresses toward being more like a Romantic, creating that same odd dynamic I described with Givers and Professors, but in reverse. This time, the Giver grows toward being more like a Romantic, and the Elegant stresses to become more like a Romantic. So in this situation, the Giver would want to help the Elegant integrate toward being more like a Player, to make it less rigid, more playful and fun, and more passionate, a more willing and inviting receiver of the Giver's giving.

If you are a Giver with an Elegant partner, you can have great sex when the Giver understands the Elegant's rules structure and adheres precisely to it, and the Elegant is complimentary because of it.

Stars

Stars are driven by their need to be the best and be perceived as the best; in appearance, accomplishment, and in lovemaking. Therefore, they are likely to be well-dressed, success-oriented, and at times superficial. Their key Facet of Sexual Expression is Growth.

What The Star Needs

Stars need to be the center of attention, to be adored, complimented, praised, and appreciated. If they don't get that reassurance from their lover, they will declare it on their own. Stars also will stop at nothing to get what they want, even deceitful behavior like cheating or lying, and then rationalizing that it wasn't that big a deal, or that they needed to do it to get ahead. So, partners of Stars need to be aware that this pattern may surface, and they'll need to be prepared to deal with it when it comes up. The Star doesn't necessarily intend to be hurtful, they just are driven to achieve at all costs, including trampling anything in their path to get there.

How the Star Sees His/Her Partner

The Star sees his or her partner as an entourage, someone who is put there to provide positive feedback and insulate and protect him or her from any negative attacks. Lovers of Stars need to be aware that the Star has a tendency toward entitlement, and some types will resent this, while others will feed into it. Let's look at how the Star interacts with each of the other types of lovers.

How the Star Interacts With the Other Types

Stars are also heart-centered types, but they tend to shut down their emotions to prevent them from interfering with the achievements the Star desires. It's no different in the sexual encounter, where the Star will do whatever it takes to get whatever he or she wants, even if someone gets hurt or is disregarded along the way.

Star-Star: In the double Star relationship, there will be conflict when one wants attention and the other is too self-absorbed to provide it, yielding great potential for mutual hostility. But double Star couples can learn to spread the adulation around, both by providing it for each other, and by finding other ways to get it. When the other ways involve another lover, there can be great capacity for deceit and evasion. But when the rewards come from work, other family members or friends, the Star couple can preserve the feelings of being special while still developing an atmosphere where both can grow. Stars stress toward being more like Dreamers, so if one or both is in stress, there can be a drag on the forward movement of the relationship. But Stars grow by becoming more like Thinkers, loyal and responsible and relationship-driven, so whoever is stronger will dictate the flow. The smart Star demonstrates love to his or her Star partner by building him or her up without need for self-aggrandizement in that particular scenario, knowing it will come later if he or she plays it well.

If you are a Star with a Star partner, you can have great sex when both feel their egos being stroked and neither feels inferior.

Star-Romantic: Stars often see their darker side in Romantics; the tragic romance, star-crossed but ill-fated, and the drama can please and titillate both—the Romantic because of the feeling of uniqueness of the relationship, and the Star because it is a target to aim at, a battle that can be won. Romantics need to be acknowledged for their individuality, while the Star needs a more general acknowledgment that the Romantic may or may not be aware of, as Romantics tend to be even more self-absorbed. Romantics stress toward being more like stressed Givers, needy and co-dependent, so the Star will need to keep his or her Romantic lover out of the doldrums by offering constant reminders of how special they are, in appearance, behavior, and lovemaking strategies. The Romantic integrates toward being more like an Elegant, so the Star can pick up on the nobility and integrity of the evolving Romantic and use it to grow toward being more like a Thinker, with more responsibility and integrity him or herself.

If you are a Star with a Romantic partner, you can have great sex when there is creative expression which makes the Star feel like the center, but acknowledges the pain the Romantic suffers because (or in spite) of it.

Star-Professor: Stars need to be sure their Professor partners are aware of their need for positive feedback, as Professors tend to be very objective and may unwittingly upset the Star by being too blunt. For example, asking, "Does my butt look fat in this dress?" will evoke an accurate assessment from a Professor, so Stars must learn not to ask questions of Professors they don't want to hear the answers to. Since Professors stress toward being more like Players, they may be more fun-loving in stress, but they are also more unpredictable, and this can be unsettling for the Star lover, who craves feedback to increase certainty, especially about their own perceived value and of course their appearance. A healthy Professor will start to resemble a Dominant, and there may be a need for some repositioning between the Star's need for acclaim and the Dominant's need for control. But the evolving Professor learns how to praise the Star and manage the situation effectively, leading to a somewhat more intellectual but often satisfying experience for the Star, and vicarious pleasure for the Professor in becoming expert in catering to the sexual needs of the Star.

If you are a Star with a Professor partner, you can have great sex when the Star feels like the center of the Professor's scientific experimentation.

Star-Thinker: Stars grow to be more like Thinkers, and Thinkers stress to be more like Stars, so whoever is stronger will dictate the flow. As with all lovers who are in each other's direction of integration and disintegration, the integrative type must show up stronger to keep the relationship healthy and moving forward. So, the Star-Thinker couple needs to stay focused more on responsibilities and engagement than on bowing to the wishes of the Star, to avoid the Thinker stressing and pushing the relationship toward a stressed double Star, a breeding ground for hostility. Another interesting dynamic is that the Thinker integrates toward the Dreamer, while the Star stresses toward the Dreamer. This means that when the Thinker grows, the Star must be aware not to slip into Dreamer tendencies. Rather, when the Thinker grows, that leaves a space for the Star to grow into, resembling a Thinker in their relationship skills and decreased edginess.

If you are a Star with a Thinker partner, you can have great sex when the Thinker comes out of his or her logical thoughts and into his or her dreams, and the Star connects with his or her emotions.

Star-Player: Stars and Players are both quite assertive, and as such may clash on the rhythms of their engagement. The Star will want the Player to revolve around him or her, while the Player will constantly seek new experiences, likely to become bored with the same patterns of adulation. So, the Star will need to keep things fresh for the Player by including new ideas, new scenarios, and new habits and behaviors. The Player requires spontaneity, so the Star will need to change up the norms to vary the sexual experiences accordingly. A new location, an interesting approach, or new attire or appearance can make it fun for the Player, so Stars have no problem dressing up, changing hairstyles, or including revolutionary ideas, as long as he or she can remain the center of attention. Players are fine with this, as long as it's fun and compelling.

Players stress toward being more like Elegants, so Stars need to look out for when their Player partners lose their flexibility or passion for new experiences, which signifies that they are stressing and need a dose of enthusiastic freshness. The Player grows by becoming more like a Professor; still curious, but expecting the answers to come from within instead of from fun and games. So when the Star sees (or orchestrates) such movement, where the Player is less flighty, less aggressive in pursuit of fun, and more internal and thoughtful, the Star can then take some credit for creating such a conducive environment, and can also expect a more thoughtful and clinically exact form of support they rarely got from the average Player.

If you are a Star with a Player partner, you can have great sex when the curiosity and adventurousness of the Player make the Star feel like the center of the world during their sexual escapades.

Star-Dominant: Stars and Dominants are the two most assertive types of lovers; the Dominant seeking control, the Star seeking acknowledgment of superiority. As such, Star-Dominant couples can have a rocky road, jockeying for power and for their own values to be met. Since the Dominant tends to think "my rules for you, no rules for me," the Star will be confronted with a choice between letting the Dominant call the shots, and subtly undermining the Dominant with deceit and hostility. The way to make a Star-Dominant relationship work is to initiate integration in the Dominant by encouraging him or her to relinquish control in favor of support, which is similar to control but orchestrates positive outcomes all can benefit from. As the Dominant integrates toward being more like a Giver, the Star gets given to, and can then let go of the hostility and self-deception.

If you are a Star with a Dominant partner, you can have great sex when the Dominant uses his or her control to support the Star's need for acknowledgment.

Star-Dreamer: Stars must remain stronger than Dreamers, or else the Star will tend to disintegrate toward being more like a Dreamer. But when the Star inspires the Dreamer to grow, the integration process makes the Dreamer more star-like, while retaining their dreamy attitudes. This causes the Dreamer to develop more drive, which can be channeled into better lovemaking and more satisfaction for the Star. The Dreamer, though, typically loves sex unconditionally, and is generally willing to do whatever it takes to please the Star, including making him or her the center of attention. Dreamers have no such interest, preferring to fly below the radar, and therefore make great lovers for Stars, as long as they have good enough appearance and prosperity to satisfy the basic needs of the Star.

If you are a Star with a Dreamer partner, you can have great sex when the Dreamer connects with the Star's need for attention and gives it freely, subtly shaping it toward the Dreamer's definition of ecstasy.

Star-Elegant: Stars expect their partners to know how to make them feel great about themselves, and Elegants are well-equipped to do so, being genteel and precise. But their civility can be tested by the Star's deceptiveness, as Elegants are determined to adhere to high standards and values—not inspired by their own rules structure, but by what they perceive to be divinely directed. While this may not be so, it seems so to the Elegant, and as such, the Star needs to avoid seeming to be outside the limits of honesty, or risk disengagement from the Elegant. But when Elegants grow, they seem more like Players, and the newfound flexibility is an opportunity for the Star to train the Elegant to be more complimentary.

If you are a Star with an Elegant partner, you can have great sex when the Elegant lightens up his or her rules structure and becomes more adventurous, constructing fun experiences that make the Star feel important and appreciated.

Star-Giver: The Star loves to be given to, and the Giver loves to give, so Star-Giver couples tend to be satisfying for both. The Star needs to be clear on how he or she wishes to be adored, and the Giver can invariably deliver. The rub comes when the Star takes without any giving back, so the smart Star will support his or her Giver lover by at least occasionally acknowledging the support and love. Surprisingly, little else is generally required, not even the follow through on the delivery of the support. The promise and the acknowledgment is often enough, at least for a long while. That promise only wears thin if there is no evidence of follow through whatsoever, and most Stars are devious enough to at least suggest the payback regularly enough to keep themselves in the limelight. The Giver will integrate toward being more like a Romantic, and as such, will be less needy and co-dependent, and more self-sufficient and individualistic. The potential danger here is that the Star will feel less supported by the independent Romantic than the supportive Giver, but if the Star also grows toward being more like a Thinker, which in this environment they often do, then they will be more responsible in the relationship.

If you are a Star with a Giver partner, you can have great sex when the Star is clear about the way he or she wishes to be made love to, and the Giver is clear on how that needs to be executed, expecting only some appreciation and approval in return.

Romantics

Romantics are focused on deep emotion, especially the darker emotions of sadness and unrequited love. Their tragic nature can make them melancholy, though they are also capable of great sexual creativity and uniqueness. Their key Facet of Sexual Expression is Beauty.

What the Romantic Needs

The Romantic needs to feel special and unique, to be different, and wave that difference as a flag. They may do this with unusual fashion, unique habits and behaviors, and often radical or off-the-beaten-track sexuality. Romantics will notice the tragic elements of relationship, the disappointments and the pain, but they will also be sensitive to the great beauty and magnificence of love at its best. This sensitivity makes them emotionally fragile at times, but also fortifies them to handle difficult circumstances when they occur.

How the Romantic Sees His/Her Partner

The Romantic will tend to see his or her partner in glorified, amplified ways. The emotions are so magnified, good things seem great, bad things seem horrible, and the measurement continues on that scale. Hence, the Romantic tends to be more extreme in his or her interpretation of everyday life, including lovemaking. The Romantic leans toward the dark side, so their partner may be regarded either as a protector from that, or a cause of it.

How the Romantic Interacts With the Other Types

Romantics are also heart-centered types, but they are so in touch with their emotions they can be held back or even injured by them. This sensitivity can manifest as fragility, sometimes leading to isolation and withdrawal, sometimes leading to bold and unique statements in attire, body adornment, and sexuality, including sexual preference and habits.

Romantic-Romantic: The double Romantic couple will be dramatic and turbulent. Each partner feels deeply, and is absorbed into the feelings. When they are happy feelings, they are ebullient, but when they are dark, they are deliciously painful and exquisitely tender. So, while having one Romantic in a relationship can make it tumultuous and afflicted, having two Romantics can put it over the top—or rather, under the bottom. Sexually, this is a place where sadomasochism may flourish. If Romantics stress too much, they start to resemble stressed Givers, so you can add co-dependency to the tragic conspiracy. But when Romantics get healthier, they start to look like Elegants; noble, clean, bright, out of the shadows. This occurs in many show business people, so often Romantics associate with noble causes as they evolve. The same thing happens in lovemaking—dark and painful patterns can be supplanted by purity and more standard, if still passionate and exciting, sexual encounters.

If you are a Romantic with a Romantic partner, you can have great sex when emotions run high, there is agreement on the degree of darkness that is appropriate, and each is allowed the space of individuality and uniqueness while they feel their way toward creating the optimal sexual package.

Romantic-Professor: Since the Romantic is so emotional and self-absorbed, a Professor will find little competition intellectually. Not because the Romantic isn't as smart, but because intellect is too exact for the abstract mind of the Romantic. This can be comforting for the Professor, but may feel stifling to both since there is such a disconnect in worldview. Still, both tend to be withdrawn, and can find space for each other; the Romantic with his or her art, the Professor with his or her science, and select places where their interests intertwine, like in odd or unusual sexual practices, role-playing, fantasy creation, and expanded sexuality. A Professor stresses to look like a Player, so the scatteredness and jittery grasping at new fun experiences can be disconcerting to the Romantic, both from genuine concern and also diversion of attention away from his or her dark worldview. But when the Professor grows to become more like a Dominant, the Romantic will feed off the certainty, and be able to integrate to seem more like an Elegant, fairness and natural rightness replacing the tragic interpretation of life and sex.

If you are a Romantic with a Professor partner, you can have great sex when the Professor takes an interest in exploring the Romantic's quirkiness, and the Romantic sees the integrity of the Professor's approach.

Romantic-Thinker: The Romantic's self-absorption and the Thinker's insecurity add up to a lot of self and mutual doubt, so Romantic-Thinker couples will need to work to develop trust. Thinkers will tend to doubt if they are adequate sexually; if they are attractive enough, if they are doing it right, if they are doing it wrong, and a litany of other thoughts that tend to keep them out of the present moment. The Romantic, on the other hand, uses the present moment as a springboard to emotional intensity, often painful, but always intended to be extreme. So, the Romantic will want to experiment with radical emotional experiences, while the Thinker will try to limit such emotional upheaval and stay in a logical train of thought. When the Thinker stresses, he or she starts to look like a Star, and the self-absorption of the Star with the depressive tendencies of the Romantic can be a volatile situation. But when the Thinker grows to be more like a Dreamer, the Romantic finds a place where fantasy and imagination can flourish, and sex becomes a more joyful and uplifting experience, especially since the Thinker retains his or her loyalty but expresses more transcendence sexually as he or she grows.

If you are a Romantic with a Thinker partner, you can have great sex when the Romantic's artistry consumes the Thinker's anxiety, and the color and excitement of the moment commandeers the Thinker into the present moment.

Romantic-Player: Players are very expressive and enthusiastic, mostly in a very upbeat way. Romantics are also expressive, but usually in a darker or more afflicted way. Put a Romantic together with a Player, and whoever is stronger will dictate the flow, manifesting as either a lighter or a darker relationship energy. Interestingly, Romantics integrate to look more like Elegants, while Players stress to become more like Elegants. So, the Romantic will need to be careful that his or her integrative energy doesn't stress the Player partner. The Romantic should concentrate on the natural rightness, and less on the rigidity and rules, and it will be less stressful for the Player.

If you are a Romantic with a Player partner, you can have great sex when the brightness of the Player integrates the darkness of the Romantic, or the individualistic and unusual interests of the Romantic intrigue and pique the curiosity of the Player, moving the Player to grow toward being more like a Professor.

Romantic-Dominant: This couple tends to be very passionate, as the Dominant will want control and the Romantic will want intense emotions to be expressed. This can lead to a thrilling but incendiary relationship, fraught with bouts of anger and hysteria, laughing and crying and everything in between; the whole spectrum of feelings. Interestingly, Dominants grow toward being more like Givers, and Romantics stress to look more like stressed Givers, so the dynamic of giving is under tension with a Romantic-Dominant couple. The Romantic wants the Dominant to integrate toward looking more like a Giver, and then must stay strong to avoid stressing in that direction.

If you're a Romantic with a Dominant partner, you can have great sex when the Romantic is expressing emotion, and the Dominant is integrating and expressing unconditional love.

Romantic-Dreamer: Dreamers are generally emotionally placid and mellow, especially by comparison to the intensity of the Romantic. So, Romantic-Dreamer couples are typically driven by the mood of the Romantic. The Dreamer, however, may act passive-aggressively toward the Romantic, not stating his or her position directly, but quietly acting it out while resisting the Romantic's emotional tides. The Dreamer is mostly well-equipped to handle the Romantic's moodiness, remaining on an even keel much of the time. But if the Dreamer stresses, he or she begins to resemble a stressed Thinker—insecure and second-guessing, which makes the emotional turbulence that much more disconcerting. But as the Dreamer integrates toward being more like a Star, capable and engaging and less comfort-driven, he or she grows and can be supportive of the Romantic's needs without being victimized by them.

If you are a Romantic with a Dreamer partner, you can have great sex when the Dreamer and the Romantic collaborate on their fantasies, and conspire to reach the heights of ecstasy together.

Romantic-Elegant: Romantics grow by becoming more like Elegants, so the key to a successful Romantic-Elegant relationship is to keep the Elegant strong so the Romantic's energy flows toward fairness and natural rightness, instead of the darker side, beautiful and enticing though it may be. If the Romantic is stronger, the couple will resemble the double Romantic couple, with emotional unrest lurking on the sidelines at all times. But with the Elegant expressing conscious standards, the Romantic is encouraged to come out of the darkness and see the beauty in other places, like higher virtues. This makes the Romantic-Elegant couple, at its best, a noble and well-adjusted pair.

If you are a Romantic with an Elegant partner, you can have great sex when the Romantic looks to the Elegant for cosmic structure, and the Romantic abstractions come into focus and perspective so they can be experienced and built upon.

Romantic-Giver: Romantics stress toward being more like Givers, so in a Romantic-Giver relationship, the Romantic must show up stronger, or risk stressing toward becoming more like a Giver, and suffering the consequences of the stressed double-Giver couple, co-dependency and vying for who can out-serve whom, and then feel hurt by not being properly appreciated. But when the Romantic is stronger, the Giver blossoms in self-sufficiency and personal growth, and they enjoy the best of the double Romantic couple, seeing beauty in everything, reaching heights of sensitivity and titillation by deeply exploring their feelings and sensations, connected but individual and independent, having a sexual communion by blending into each other while retaining their identities.

If you are a Romantic with a Giver partner, you can have great sex when the Romantic is strong enough to direct the flow. When the Giver is willing to follow the Romantic's lead, even if it means unusual tastes, fetishes or the dark side, all he or she needs to stay engaged is acknowledgment.

Romantic-Star: Romantics and Stars are at opposite ends of the emotional spectrum. Romantics feel deeply, and Stars avoid feeling because it risks distraction from being the best. So, Stars may be impatient with Romantics, who seem like they are too subject to their own feelings, something Stars have learned not to do. When faced repeatedly with the Romantic's emotional roller coaster, Stars may stress toward being like Dreamers, withdrawing and going into a personal dream world that avoids confrontation and reality. On the other hand, when the Romantic is exposed to the Star's drive, it can seem too linear and simplistic, whereas the artistic viewpoint the Romantic enjoys would have more color and scope. As these two are the most self-absorbed types, the subtlety of making this relationship work revolves around the Star recognizing the Romantic's beauty and uniqueness, and the Romantic recognizing the Star's need to be at the center.

If you are a Romantic with a Star partner, you can have great sex when you conspire to delve into the fantasies of the Romantic, while developing a platform for the Star to shine.

Professors

Professors are focused on intellect and systems, and their interest in sexuality can seem detached or withdrawn—even, well, professorial. But they are highly vulnerable on the inside, and use their knowledge as a shield of arrogance to hide behind, avoiding all but the most desirable and necessary connections. Their key Facet of Sexual Expression is Wisdom.

What the Professor Needs

The Professor needs to stake an intellectual claim to a particular area of study. In lovemaking, it could be a specific fetish, a ritual or habit, or a little-known technique that creates some special sexual result, like squirting or anal orgasms. Professors need to feel and look smart, and their lovers need to know how to challenge them without escalation, which would decrease connection and drive sexual engagement further away.

How the Professor Sees His/Her Partner

The Professor sees his or her world like an opportunity for scientific inquiry, noticing distinctions and details about their surroundings and cataloguing them for future application. In the sexual encounter, this makes the Professor a wonderful older partner, using experience and wisdom to guide someone younger and less likely to create conflict. So, a Professor often sees his or her partner as a student or assistant.

How the Professor Interacts With the Other Types

Because the head-centered Professor never wants to be seen as not knowing, especially in his or her area of expertise or mastery, he or she will often stake out a territory and expect not to be challenged in that area, doing everything possible to be thoroughly well-versed. It could be a sexual specialty, like a favorite oral sex technique, a method of delaying ejaculation, or an exotic approach from other cultures or other eras. So, the Professor tends to develop relationships carefully, preserving the intellectual pecking order, and only engaging slowly and after significant trust has been established, especially given the odd sexual tastes that sometimes manifest.

Professor-Professor: When two Professors get together, it's essential to divide up the intellectual landscape, or else the battle for supremacy will consume the relationship's energy, leaving them too exhausted to share and enjoy the finer things. So, the smart Professor maneuvers toward assignment of territories for each to reign over, yielding to the other's opinion when necessary, according to the organizing principles that are developed. When one or both is in stress, they'll start to resemble stressed Players; scattered, imprecise, and demonstrating an uncharacteristically short attention span, starting but not finishing before losing interest. But when Professors grow, they show up more like Dominants—certain, secure, forthright but not arrogant, centered instead of intellectually defensive. At their best, double Professor couples are wise and well-orchestrated, with their sexual tastes and idiosyncrasies worked out and accommodated systematically and accurately.

If you are a Professor with a Professor partner, you can have great sex when each Professor chooses an area of expertise and plays it out, with full buy-in from the other Professor.

Professor-Thinker: Professors and Thinkers are both head-centered, but the Thinker's insecurities are generalized, whereas the Professor's doubts are crystallized around their intellectual pursuits. So, the Professor who wants his or her Thinker partner to relax provides certainty in their areas of expertise, allowing the Thinker to doubt less in those specific areas, earning the Professor some latitude and freedom. Thinkers are loyal and willing, up to a point; but it is hard for them to stay present, since they tend to gain more certainty by filtering their current moment through their past reference experiences, observing how this new moment is like something they feel they already understand. This drives the Thinker out of the moment, so the Professor must find ways to instigate and preserve engagement, and in a healthy state, is generally up to the task.

If you are a Professor with a Thinker partner, you can have great sex when the Professor can find a way to occupy the Thinker's mind, and engage them in their specialty to provide certainty and an opportunity for the Thinker to trust the Professor and let go.

Professor-Player: The Professor and the Player are both head-centered, and have the advantage of being in each other's direction of integration and disintegration. In other words, the Player grows by becoming more like the Professor, and when the Professor stresses, he or she shows up more like a stressed Player. So, the relationship grows when the Professor is stronger, and the Player evolves to discover passion and excitement inside, rather than only in new adventures and experiences. This transforms the insatiability of the Player into a feeling of all-knowingness, as the Professor replaces knowledge with wisdom, success with fulfillment, and health with wellness.

If you are a Professor with a Player partner, you can have great sex when the Professor stays stronger than the Player, harnessing the adventurousness, guiding it with sensibility, and channeling it into the potency of the relationship, the reflection of all of their attention.

Professor-Dominant: Professors grow by becoming more like Dominants, so when the Dominant is stronger, the Professor will tend to integrate, become more certain and less arrogant. While he or she will still be dedicated to being expert in niche areas, the integration process brings a more global orientation, in life and sexually, too. Professors don't just accept the control of the Dominant, but if the Dominant is consistent, the Professor comes out of logic and moves into an instinctive sexual place, similar to the Dominant. Then, the couple can enjoy a passionate and powerful sexual exchange.

If you are a Professor with a Dominant partner, you can have great sex when the Professor allows the Dominant to lead, leaving intellectual arrogance behind in favor of a centered, grounded lovemaking experience.

Professor-Dreamer: Dreamers will tend to yield to the intellectual certainty of the Professor, preferring to avoid confrontation, and will usually go along with the Professor's odd tastes and peculiarities without too much overt conflict. But the Dreamer needs his or her dreams to be fulfilled too, and only when the Dreamer grows enough to voice his or her desires will the Professor be likely to respond. The Dreamer is very body-centered, and Professors will do well to learn their erogenous zones and reach them physically, letting go of the need to manage through their minds.

If you are a Professor with a Dreamer partner, you can have great sex when you find the interface between the Dreamer's imagination and physical desires, and the Professor's area of expertise.

Professor-Elegant: Professors and Elegants both have strong self-images; Professors based on their perception of their intellect, and Elegants based on their perception of universal truth. This can cause a clash between ideologies that can carry into the bedroom. So, the Professor-Elegant couple is best off arranging for systematic rules that define the appropriate behaviors in typical circumstances. Committing to leaving spirited debate out of lovemaking, or finding a way to incorporate it as stimulating foreplay will pave the way toward improved intimacy even in the face of any potential philosophical divergence. At best, though, the Elegant evolves to look more like a Player, and the Professor resists the pull of Playerness that would stress him or her, leaving a flexible and playful Elegant to entertain the Professor, making him or her happier.

If you are a Professor with an Elegant partner, you can have great sex when the Professor creates a safe frame for the Elegant to be more curious and adventurous, and the Professor guides him or her through the willingness to let go and experience new adventures without becoming scattered.

Professor-Giver: Professors grow towards powerful Dominant energy, and Givers stress toward it. Professor-Giver couples can have volatile relationships unless either or both decide to tap into the certainty the Professor develops, while the Giver keeps giving and feeding the evolving Professor with love and support, bringing out his or her Dominant leader energy. Professors may start out arrogant when they are getting used to a new relationship, as a protective device, but they can quickly learn the Giver's giving patterns, systematize the appropriate responses that evoke the desired behaviors, and make the Giver feel appreciated and fulfilled.

If you are a Professor with a Giver partner, you can have great sex when the Professor optimizes the Giver's willingness to provide sexual pleasure when they feel compensated and rewarded for their love.

Professor-Star: Professors and Stars may find themselves vying for position, competing intellectually and physically. Professors are accustomed to being on top intellectually, and Stars are just accustomed to being on top. So, when the Star stresses, he or she will withdraw, recoiling from the Professor's arrogance. The Professor must the tone it down, make the Star the center of attention again, and resist the impulse to be right.

If you are a Professor with a Star partner, you can have great sex when the Professor releases the need to dictate terms, and rather, makes the Star the most important thing, even if it's with a wink.

Professor-Romantic: While the Professor will have precise scientific knowledge, the Romantic will have abstract and artistic license. This makes for a bit of a wrestling match between mind and heart. Since the Romantic may focus on the dark side, the Professor may become intrigued with the same and develop it as a course of study, becoming expert. This can make for a unique but systematic lovemaking, often based on ritual, fetish, and ceremony.

If you are a Professor with a Romantic partner, you can have great sex when the Professor feeds the Romantic's emotional needs systematically and precisely, maneuvering into his or her desired scenarios.

Thinkers

Thinkers are constantly consumed with their thoughts. Their minds are never quiet, with the intention of consistently scanning the horizon for danger, quickly comparing what they observe to that which they have already experienced to gain an edge on staying safe. The trade-off is that they are never present, since they run the present moment through past reference experiences for evaluation and ongoing filing. They are loyal, responsible, and generally willing lovers, but it's difficult for them to fully engage because of these tendencies. Their key Facet of Sexual Expression is Security.

What the Thinker Needs

The Thinker needs security above all, and has trouble feeling secure even when conditions are favorable. This makes them anxious, which detracts from their lovemaking experience. The sexual encounter becomes an opportunity for self-judgment and nitpicking, which is usually not as much about what their lover is doing as it is about the moving target of the Thinker's own pleasure.

How the Thinker Sees His/Her Partner

Thinkers see their partners as teammates, aligned but separate. They believe that no one can see the world as acutely as they do, since their vigilance has life or death consequences in their minds. This is head-centeredness gone astray, and the average to unhealthy Thinker can be paranoid, questioning everything, and sometimes inventing things to be worried about, to the detriment of their partner's inner peace.

How the Thinker Interacts With the Other Types

Thinkers use thinking and questioning as a defense mechanism to interpret and protect themselves from their realities. The exchanges are largely linguistic, as Thinkers are caught in their thoughts, and their feelings are most accessible when they stress, so they can come across as neurotic. But evolving Thinkers can be solid relationship mates; trustworthy, faithful, and able to go outside their boundaries, with enough patience and support.

Thinker-Thinker: When two Thinkers create a relationship, there will be logic and reason at the forefront. Since both are so security-minded, it's unlikely that too many chances will be taken. Rather, they will forge a predictable and somewhat cautious existence, often with predictable and cautious sex. This couple will avoid risk, though as they grow, they will become more like Dreamers, and perhaps will be willing to push the envelope in the direction of their fantasies.

If you are a Thinker with a Thinker partner, you can have great sex when you get your lover out of his or her mind and into his or her body, with gentle conversation that tapers off as the physicality begins, and with gentle and patient physical engagement that manifests as the Thinker letting go of thought in favor of instinctual responses and positive sensations.

Thinker-Player: Thinkers and Players are both head-centered types, but they approach it from opposite perspectives. The Thinker intends to stay safe by carefully measuring everything they can detect in their environment, and the Player casts fate to the wind and tries to experience everything possible in their environment. They are both processing their fears, but the Thinker does it by considering, and the Player by plunging through. So, when one lover has a high value on security, and the other on adventure, it can require significant negotiation to come to common ground.

If you are a Thinker with a Player partner, you can have great sex when the Thinker fastens his or her seatbelt and gets ready for a fun ride. The Player wants new, fun and passionate experiences, and the Thinker is best served by integrating toward a place of calm and inner peace, and hanging on for dear life while the Player explores and experiences.

Thinker-Dominant: Often, the Thinker seeks security by connecting with a Dominant, who excels at certainty. In Thinker-Dominant couples, the Thinker tends to relinquish control to the Dominant, sometimes leading to bondage, or at least fantasy role-play that features and contrasts the differing worldviews. Dominants come from "my rules for you, no rules for me," while Thinkers question all rules but succumb to many or most of them, for fear of being disloyal or out of alignment.

If you are a Thinker with a Dominant partner, you can have great sex when the Thinker lets the Dominant take the lead, and offers his or her input as shaping and guidance rather than foundational. The Dominant wants to call the shots, and smart Thinkers learn how to be heard within that directive flow.

Thinker-Dreamer: This is also a very common configuration, as Thinkers integrate toward being more like Dreamers, stilling their internal dialogue and developing inner peace as opposed to overcerebrating turmoil. The Dreamer must stay stronger than the Thinker, or else the Dreamer stresses and goes into his or her thoughts, which only amplifies the Thinker's insecurities. But when the Dreamer is strong, the Thinker uses him or her as a role model and comes to a place of inner quiet, at least by comparison, and that allows the Thinker to be more present in the lovemaking scenario.

If you are a Thinker with a Dreamer partner, you can have great sex when the Thinker quiets his or her internal dialogue based on the Dreamer's role model, and becomes more present in the moment when making love, in the body instead of the mind.

Thinker-Elegant: Thinkers and Elegants frequently have similar boundaries, but for different reasons. The Elegant is seeking consistency with universal laws, while the Thinker is seeking safety and protection. Still, both will tend to find a love-making style and habit that doesn't push beyond their versions of propriety. In an average place, their lovemaking could be dull or predictable. But as the Elegant grows toward being more like a Player, and as the Thinker grows to be more like a Dreamer, their lovemaking can take on substantial thrills, more like a Dreamer-Player couple (see below).

If you are a Thinker with an Elegant partner, you can have great sex when you lighten up, create a more playful scenario, and clearly define the boundaries in advance, so everyone is comfortable with the rules structure and can partici-pate without overanalysis.

Thinker-Giver: Thinkers and Givers are among the most compliant lovers, both willing to honor the other's wishes, even past a point of some discomfort. So, Thinker-Giver couples are usually very civil, very supportive of each other, and have the potential for hot lovemaking, especially if the Thinker is evolving toward being more like a Dreamer, providing a series of wonderful fantasies for the Giver to work toward satisfying. Avoid allowing the Thinker to become stronger than the Giver, which could stress the Giver to become more like a Dominant, who would then commandeer the relationship. If this happens, the Thinker can simply engage the Giver's help on something, and the Giver snaps back into an average-to-healthy place.

If you are a Thinker with a Giver partner, you can have great sex when the Thinker allows the Giver to give, releasing the insecurity enough to respond to the Giver's efforts in the current moment, so good times can follow.

Thinker-Star: Since Stars integrate to become more like Thinkers, and Thinkers stress to become more like Stars, this couple has to keep the Thinker strong so the Star can grow instead of the Thinker stressing. If the Star gets stronger, then the hostility will mount, and the Thinker will become more ego-driven and self-conscious. This starts to resemble a Star-Star relationship, where there will be competitive jockeying for position, so whoever notices this pattern first should run to a place of connection, loyalty, and kindness.

If you are a Thinker with a Star partner, you can have great sex when the Thinker remains strong to keep the Star integrating, so it becomes less about perceptions and appearances, and more about substance and genuine engagement.

Thinker-Romantic: The Thinker processes with thoughts, and the Romantic processes with feelings, so it can be difficult for them to get on the same page, even to be speaking the same language. The key is in growth and integration, where the Thinker evolves in the direction of being more like a Dreamer, and the Romantic evolves in a direction of being more like an Elegant. Now, the Thinker is less driven by thoughts and more by instincts, and the Romantic is less governed by emotions and more by universal principles. This is a more conducive environment for quality lovemaking, where they can both be present in the moment, and the Dreamer-like fantasies and loosening boundaries can help the evolving Romantic to be less a victim of his or her emotions and more a skillful agent who utilizes them.

If you are a Thinker with an Elegant partner, you can have great sex when the Thinker releases his or her stranglehold on thoughts and begins to dream, which inspires the Romantic partner to also dream and uncover positive sensations and desires.

Thinker-Professor: This is one of the most intellectual couples, with the lust for knowledge of the Professor leading the Thinker to overthink. Since both are quite head-centered, a verbal, intellectual, and thought-driven sexuality can work wonders with such a couple. These lovers must talk about and define their desires, maintaining rapport and committing not to overreact. By discovering each other's wants and needs, they can come to agreement on what lovemaking endeavors are satisfying for each and both, and come up with a structure that enthuses both.

If you are a Thinker with a Professor partner, the Thinker must position the Professor as the expert, so there is no intellectual competition, and the Thinker must claim a space for inserting his or her desires, which the Professor must commit to supporting. The finesse comes in the Thinker framing his or her desires as part of the Professor's model of lovemaking, in which case it is easily included.

Players

Players are fun-loving, enthusiastic and playful, but they tend to have short attention spans and bore easily. This makes it more difficult for them to maintain a committed relationship, often preferring multiple lovers or short-term relationships. They are among the most expressive lovers, as they love to squeeze all the juice out of life and sex. Their key Facet of Sexual Expression is Passion.

What the Player Needs

Players need variety, spontaneity, and activities that are interesting and fun. They abhor boredom and dullness, and are constantly moving forward, looking for new adventures and experiences.

How the Player Sees His/Her Partner

The Player sees his or her partner as a vehicle to excitement, and as long as this is true, the Player can stay in relationship. But if they get bored, unhappy, or just distracted, they can be off and running toward new, cool stuff for them to experience.

How the Player Interacts With the Other Types

Because the Player has a short attention span, relationships sometimes self-limit based on the Player's level of desire to follow through. If they have a compelling future, it can work long term, but many times does not. But because Players are so much fun to be around, they rarely lack for company, though the engagement may be brief by comparison.

Player-Player: The double Player couple is tons of fun, but their mutual desire for newness often drives them apart before too long. The best chance a Player-Player relationship may have is when one or both begin to grow toward being more like Professors, so the lust for adventure is sublimated into a realization that excitement dwells within. This can make the Player more sedate and less aggressive in pursuit of external experiences.

If you are a Player with a Player partner, you can have great sex when one or both Players thoughtfully considers the option of seeking adventure inside, instead of as a product of constant forward thrust.

Player-Dominant: One of the most assertive configurations possible, the Player-Dominant couple has the interesting dynamic that the Player grows to be more like a Professor, while the Dominant stresses to look more like a Professor. So, a smart Player will allow the Dominant to retain control, even as he or she grows to discover greatness and passion inside. The Dominant can then grow to become more like a Giver, who can then keep pace with the many desires of the evolving Player.

If you are a Player with a Dominant partner, you can have great sex when the Player encourages the Dominant to be more loving, and therefore more compliant with the adventure-lust of the Player.

Player-Dreamer: These can be fun and adventurous couples, because the Dreamer is generally willing to go along with whatever the Player wants, as long as there is some room for the Dreamer's dreams, too. So, Player-Dreamer relationships are filled with joyful activities, randy sex, perhaps pushing the boundaries with extreme sexual practices such as polyamory, same-sex experiences, swinging, and other subtle and not-so-subtle over-the-line behaviors.

If you are a Player with a Dreamer partner, you can have great sex when the Player encourages the Dreamer to participate in his or her fantasies, and the Dreamer encourages the Player to participate in his or hers. This makes for a fun ride for all concerned.

Player-Elegant: Players stress to look more like Elegants, and Elegants grow to look more like Players. So, in a Player-Elegant couple, the Player must remain strong to prevent him or herself from stressing toward the Elegant, and to grow the Elegant to be more playful, fun and spontaneous, with fewer rules that could be violated by rowdy or sexy behaviors. Elegants will tend to want to maintain their boundaries, which makes it all that much more important for the Player to keep rapport and elicit values to move the Elegant in an integrative direction. Otherwise, the Player will stress toward the Elegant's patterns, become stifled and unhappy, and usually terminate the relationship in hopes of finding something more entertaining.

If you are a Player with an Elegant partner, you can have great sex when the Player encourages the Elegant to lighten up his or her rules structure and fully engage the fun activities the Player craves.

Player-Giver: This couple is also often very fun, since the Player looks for fun and the Giver looks to support his or her partner. Therefore, the Player-Giver relationship is entertaining, as long as both partners keep growing and moving forward. If the Player stresses to look more like an Elegant, the rules will tighten around which kinds of help and support the Giver can offer, based on the Players now-distorted interpretation. Also, if the Giver stresses to become more like a Dominant, that control will interfere with the Player's desires to be footloose and fancy-free, risking the relationship's viability. But when the Giver becomes less co-dependent and moves toward being more like a Romantic, and the Player grows toward wisdom by becoming more like a Professor, the relationships comes out of its self-indulgence and integrates like a Professor-Romantic couple, based on sound organizing principles and available to both in a constructive and healthy format.

If you are a Player with a Giver partner, you can have great sex when the Player shapes his or her adventure around the Giver's need to help and support. When the Giver plays a significant role in the Player's adventures, great sex happens naturally.

Player-Star: The Star's self-absorption can challenge the Player's need for variety. If the Star always needs to be the center of attention, the Player will feel stifled and unable to execute on his or her worldview of excitement. So, the Player needs to structure his or her adventures around the Star's self-image of being the best. Both are quite assertive, and will vie for the space that is available. The key is for the Player to proactively support the Star's need to be adored, and make it part of the play of life the Player is constantly acting in.

If you are a Player with a Star partner, you can have great sex when the Player creates playtime the Star can engage in and feel an integral part of, soothing his or her need to be at the center of things.

Player-Romantic: Interestingly, the Romantic grows to become more like an Elegant, and the Player stresses to look more like a stressed Elegant. These are dangerous patterns, because neither the Player nor the Romantic responds especially well to rules being established for them, preferring to evolve their rules structure themselves. So, as the Romantic grows and establishes a more finite, less abstract reality for themselves, the Player must carefully avoid stressing, staying upbeat, and focused on new experiences.

If you are a Player with a Romantic partner, you can have great sex when the Player creates fun experiences that grow the Romantic out of his or her darkness and into the glow of natural rightness and universal law. The Player grows toward being more Professor-like, and will find the evolved Romantic an able relationship mate with these patterns exposed.

Player-Professor: Players integrate toward being more like Professors, so this relationship can be ideal for a Player, with a constant reminder of what health and wellness look like. The Professor must stay stronger than the Player, though, or else the opposite will occur. The Professor will stress toward the Player, becoming scattered, losing detail orientation, and getting consumed with desire for fresh experiences instead of using current knowledge as a platform to push up from.

If you are a Player with a Professor partner, you can have great sex when the Player lets the Professor lead the way, and creates a pathway to an inner excitement instead of feeling like fun is outside him or herself.

Player-Thinker: Players and Thinkers are both head-centered types, but Players think quickly and briefly, while Thinkers overcerebrate and overanalyze. Add to the mix the values discrepancy, where Players value adventure and Thinkers value security, and you can see the built-in rub. Thinkers want to play it close to the vest, and Players want to let it all hang out. As both types move toward sexual wellness, the Player by being more Professor-like and the Thinker by being more Dreamer-like, the patterns combine better. As in a Professor-Dreamer couple, the evolving Player leads with wisdom, and the evolving Thinker follows, blending without undue overcerebration.

If you are a Player with a Thinker partner, you can have great sex when the Player guides the Thinker out of his or her head and into the present moment, and the Player learns to find ecstasy inside instead of on the fly.

Dominants

Dominants are strong and powerful, the most assertive of all types of lovers, believing they have the right to set rules for others and decide whether or not to follow them themselves. This "my rules for you, no rules for me" style can push people's buttons. Dominants have big energy fields, taking up most of the available space, wanting things their way. Their key Facet of Sexual Expression is Strength.

What the Dominant Needs

The Dominant needs control, to harness the people and things in their environment and have them dance to the Dominant's drumbeat. Their anger is close to the surface, and they can use it as a weapon to retain control.

How the Dominant Sees His/Her Partner

Dominants tend to regard partners as property, or pawns in their personal chess game. Instinctually, Dominants are leaders, and use this orientation to manage those around them to act consistently with the Dominant's worldview.

How the Dominant Interacts With the Other Types

The Dominant's nature is to use all resources to support his or her reality, to control the environment and everyone in it to the greatest degree possible.

Dominant-Dominant: The double Dominant couple must divide up the territory or risk being in constant conflict. Unless the domains are well-defined, they will squabble over boundaries, and ultimately destroy the relationship. But when they are willing to come to negotiated terms on who controls what, they can move forward together. One or both must integrate toward showing up more like a Giver, so that unconditional love begins to permeate the relationship instead of just control. The willingness to do for each other evolves out of this integration process.

If you are a Dominant with a Dominant partner, you can have great sex when at least one Dominant grows toward the Giver's lovingness and is willing to relinquish control for long enough for the love to take hold.

Dominant-Dreamer: This is another common configuration, because the Dreamer is usually fine with being controlled, up to a point. If that point is surpassed, the Dreamer gets passive-aggressive and finds ways to undermine the Dominant's control. But usually, the Dreamer just allows the Dominant to call the shots, preferring to coast and be guided along by the stronger partner.

If you are a Dominant with a Dreamer partner, you can have great sex when the Dominant is clear with the Dreamer about what is expected, and the Dreamer has enough of his or her dream included in the Dominant's rules structure to stay on board.

Dominant-Elegant: The Dominant-Elegant couple can clash because both are quite dedicated to their own respective rules structure; the Dominant to his or her own rules, and the Elegant to universal or natural laws. It's interesting that the Dominant derives his or her own rules hierarchies, and in many ways so does the Elegant, though he or she believes it was inspired from on high. This divine interpretation of their worldview makes it difficult for Elegants to relinquish their priorities to the Dominant's control. But when the Dominant grows to be more like a Giver, he or she can meet the standards of the Elegant and contribute to a passionate and productive relationship, especially when the Elegant integrates to be more flexible, like a Player.

If you are a Dominant with an Elegant partner, you can have great sex by growing to be more like a Giver and expressing love unconditionally, and help the Elegant grow toward being more like a Player so fun, passion, and adventure become part of the mix.

Dominant-Giver: This is the easiest relationship for the Dominant to flourish in, as long as the Giver is strong enough to keep the Dominant from overpowering him or her. When the Giver provides an integrative role model of love and giving, the Dominant tends to move in that direction, making the couple resemble a double Giver couple with love free-flowing and satisfying for all involved.

If you are a Dominant with a Giver partner, you can have great sex when the Dominant allows the Giver to be stronger, so the Giver's lovingness directs the flow and inspires the Dominant to also be more giving and loving.

Dominant-Star: This is a more difficult configuration, as the Dominant wants to be in control, and the Star wants to be the center of attention. If this relationship is to work, then the Dominant must grow to become more giving, and the Star must grow to become more like a Thinker, loyal and responsible. The Star's self-absorption will anger the Dominant, and the Dominant's controlling attitudes will disrespect the Star, so both must work toward integration to have a chance of making it work.

If you are a Dominant with a Star partner, the Dominant must find ways to make his or her control support the Star's need for accolades and attention. As the Dominant grows toward being more like a Giver, unconditional love and support will manifest, making it more palatable to honor the Star's need for adulation.

Dominant-Romantic: This is a turbulently passionate configuration. The controlling nature of the Dominant conflicts with the emotional roller coaster of the Romantic. The Romantic is controlling in his or her own way, using emotions as a weapon to shape his or her reality. But the Dominant has not time or patience for such games. Dominants are very black and white, just as Romantics are very sensitive to shades of color and difference. But both tend to be extreme in executing their patterns of behavior. So, this relationship works best when the Romantic grows toward being more like an Elegant, seeing the natural rightness in things, while the Dominant grows to be more like a Giver, seeing the opportunities to be more loving and helpful.

If you are a Dominant with a Romantic partner, you can have great sex when the Dominant harnesses the passion of his or her anger, and the Romantic commandeers the intensity of his or her emotion, and they throw it together to make a passionate and tumultuous and highly orgasmic relationship.

Dominant-Professor: Dominants stress to look more like Professors, and Professors grow to look more like Dominants, so there is great potential for this relationship when the Dominant remains stronger so the Professor integrates. The more the Dominant feels the Professor growing the more likely that the Dominant can then evolve toward being more like a Giver, and then in that configuration there is greater capacity for lovemaking success.

If you are a Dominant with a Professor partner, you can have great sex when the Dominant stays strong so the Professor is compelled to integrate, holding that space so the Dominant can evolve toward being more like a Giver. Then, the couple looks more like a Giver-Dominant relationship, making it easier to exchange loving sensations and behaviors.

Dominant-Thinker: Dominants tend to attract Thinkers, whose insecurity is addressed nicely by the Dominant's certainty. The Thinker is fine with releasing the decision-making to the Dominant, whose control may irk the Thinker, but not enough to buck it. The Thinker's loyalty dovetails well with the Dominant's leadership, and Dominant-Thinker couples usually last long term, as the Thinker wants to be part of the Dominant's vision, and the Dominant needs soldiers to carry out his or her bidding. In the lovemaking scenario, the Dominant is invariably in control, often requiring the Thinker to go beyond his or her boundaries, but generally willing to do so in the name of duty. Thinkers in this context are troopers, hanging in there and doing what it takes to keep the Dominant happy, or at least not angry.

If you are a Dominant with a Thinker partner, you can have great sex when the Dominant grows to be more like a Giver, retaining a controlling attitude, but using it to produce an unconditionally loving environment where the Thinker can grow to become more like a Dreamer, come out of his or her head to engage in the present moment, and become available to support the Dominant in being more giving and loving.

Dominant-Player: The Dominant-Player couple can be difficult, in that the Dominant wants control, and the Player is the strongest at resisting control, preferring freedom of movement and latitude to pursue excitement on his or her terms. These relationships work best when the Dominant grows to be more like a Giver, who then better tolerates the Player's wildness and variety-lust. The Dominant still doesn't like not being able to control the Player, but accepts that it comes along with the territory when love and support are driving the experience instead of control and anger.

If you are a Dominant with a Player partner, you can have great sex by being entertained by the Player's escapades instead of offended by them. When the Dominant integrates toward becoming more like a Giver, this pattern is easier to develop and maintain, as unconditional love makes the Player's inconsistencies charming instead of exasperating.

Dreamers

Dreamers detach from the world around them in favor of an internal fantasy world where pleasure is abundant and confrontation is rarely required. They are habitual, rhythmic, and consistent, navigating carefully to avoid conflict and maximize comfort. As such, they often underachieve, preferring to coast on past successes rather than strive to be the best they could be. This makes them pleasant enough to be around, but they engage their environment with only a small portion of their consciousness, preserving the rest to float around inside their heads. They have a highly developed sexual fantasy machine, but usually default to their imagination, since actual engagement would require too much energy, confrontation, and discomfort. Their key Facet of Sexual Expression is Harmony.

What the Dreamer Needs

The Dreamer is placid and nice on the surface, but underneath is a seething volcano of anger, which the Dreamer squashes down instead of expressing it in a healthy fashion. This makes the Dreamer passive-aggressive, letting his or her anger seep out instead of clearly and directly expressing it. Dreamers need a peaceful environment so there is less risk of their anger boiling over.

Dreamers also are body-centered, and physicality is a high value for them. They love their sex, but also have a well-developed fantasy mechanism, their salvation when pursuing real sex is too much trouble or too challenging.

How the Dreamer Sees His/Her Partner

The Dreamer usually sees his or her partner as the overt leader of the relationship, as Dreamers often show up submissive. Their passive-aggressiveness makes them stubborn, though, so they can be pleasant on the outside while remaining obstinate on the inside. They may see their partners as adversaries who could disrupt their comfort.

How the Dreamer Interacts With the Other Types

The Dreamer tends to be malleable and flexible, usually willing to go along with anything reasonable. This willingness originates with a poor self-image, as young Dreamers often question their own self-worth and right to an opinion. This makes them good team players, as their sense of ego does not require them to be at the helm, or even to be fully heard. In relationship, this makes Dreamers easygoing, but beneath their calm exterior is a fantasy world of their own design and construction, often with creature comforts like sex, food, and intoxicants over-prioritized.

Dreamer-Dreamer: When two Dreamers get together, a gradient of possibilities are available, from absolute inactivity to the mutual development of drive and purpose that spurs them to productivity in life and in their lovemaking, Either way, though, double Dreamer couples will do it, as often and as much as they can. Dreamers are pleasure freaks, and if they have a willing partner, which another Dreamer surely is, they can default to the pure pleasures of sex as another of their addictions. If one or the other stresses toward being more like a stressed Thinker, they will come out of their bodies and get stuck in their heads, until they do something rhythmic and habitual to get back into an average place. But when one or the other Dreamer grows toward being more like a Star, the drive makes them more effective and competent at whatever they do, at work, in the family, and in bed.

If you are a Dreamer with a Dreamer partner, you can have great sex when either or both Dreamers choose sexual outcomes to work toward, and develop the drive and self-discipline to pursue them instead of just defaulting to typical comforts.

Dreamer-Elegant: The Dreamer-Elegant couple is mostly defined by the Elegant's rules, as the Dreamer will usually not overtly confront the Elegant, but inside there may be resentment or acquiescence, depending on how oppressed the Dreamer feels. As long as the Dreamer has his or her inner world, the outer engagement takes less energy and attention, unless the Elegant insists on it. So, usually their sexuality is somewhat rigid and predictable, as the Dreamer will let the Elegant set the boundaries. But over time, the Dreamer may be able to insert his or her prime wants and needs, as the Elegant will see the natural rightness of allowing them to become part of their sexual practice.

If you are a Dominant with an Elegant partner, you can have great sex when the Dreamer uses the leverage of universal law to open up the Elegant to the bodily pleasures that the Dreamer excels in.

Dreamer-Giver: Dreamers love having Giver partners, since they are willing to do whatever. In many relationships, the Dreamer is the more submissive. But with a Giver, who enjoys and lives for serving the needs of others, the Dreamer has carte blanche to expect whatever sexual peculiarities his or her twisted little mind can come up with, and usually the Giver will comply. As the Dreamer integrates toward being more Star-like, drive and determination will manifest to replace the complacency and mediocrity of the average Dreamer. By emerging from his or her shell and becoming present with his or her opportunities, in life and sexually, the Dreamer can lead the Giver to an ecstatic and thoroughly enjoyable sexuality.

If you are a Dreamer with a Giver partner, you can have great sex when the Dreamer asks the Giver specifically for what he or she wants, and then grows to lead the Giver toward a higher vibration of lovemaking, remembering to appreciate and acknowledge the Giver along the way.

Dreamer-Star: Dreamers integrate by becoming more like Stars, so the key to the Dreamer-Star couple is that the Star must remain strong so the Dreamer grows toward him or her. If the Dreamer is stronger, the Star will stress, get hostile, and before too long, disengage. As long as the Star is stronger, the Dreamer will feel compelled to develop drive, both in life and sexually. Because the Star wants to be the center of attention, and the Dreamer is happy to comply with that, they can have very hot lovemaking sessions, with the Dreamer acting out fantasies by enthusiastically servicing the Star.

If you are a Dreamer with a Star partner, you can have great sex when the Star is stronger, the Dreamer grows toward the Star, and both develop drive to excel sexually in the bedroom, not merely in the Dreamer's imagination.

Dreamer-Romantic: Dreamer-Romantic couples have a great capacity for unique and unusual sexual practices. Both can be immensely creative, and the Romantic's self-absorption and tendency to see the dark side can shape the Dreamer's fantasy world, leaving them together to explore the taboo sexuality many wouldn't risk.

If you are a Dreamer with a Romantic partner, you can have great sex when the Dreamer is willing to share his or her perspectives with the Romantic, so they can work together to create ecstasy and sexual fulfillment.

Dreamer-Professor: Dreamers will tend to yield to the caustic and arrogant tone of the Professor, but may harbor resentment if they don't have a chance to carve out a place for themselves. So, the Dreamer can look for patterns of pleasure and stimulation in the Professor's area of expertise, and when there's a good fit, there can be satisfying and meaningful lovemaking. Since Dreamers often have a wide range of acceptable in their sexuality, they can usually find some aspect of the Professor's interest that works for them.

If you are a Dreamer with a Professor partner, you can have great sex when the Dreamer fits his or her dreams to the Professor's specialty.

Dreamer-Thinker: Dreamer-Thinker couples are very common, as the Thinker finds a way toward security through the inner peace of the Dreamer. But the Dreamer must remain the stronger, or else risk stressing toward the Thinker and becoming insecure and indecisive. Also, the loyalty and relationship-consciousness of the

Thinker makes him or her a willing participant in the acting out of the Dreamer's inner world. As such, they usually have very active sex lives.

If you are a Dreamer with a Thinker partner you can have great sex when the Dreamer is stronger, and helps the Thinker come out of his or her head and get into his or her body.

Dreamer-Player: The Dreamer is generally well-equipped to keep up with the adventurousness of the Player, though the Player often operates at a much quicker pace than the more laid back and internal Dreamer. The energy and vitality of the Player often integrates the Dreamer to become more Star-like, and that drive and assertiveness is helpful so the Dreamer can keep up with the Player.

If you are a Dreamer with a Player partner, you can have great sex when the Dreamer increases his or her pace to stay engaged with the more enthusiastic, more colorful, more passionate Player.

Dreamer-Dominant: In the Dreamer-Dominant couple, you have the most assertive type juxtaposed with the most submissive type. The Dreamer is generally content to let the Dominant retain control. And as long as the Dominant is a benevolent leader, the Dreamer can coast merrily along. But if the pressure of the controlling methodology of the Dominant proves to be too much for the Dreamer, he or she will shut down and go inside, until there is a space that matches his or her dream available to experience. So, the Dominant must integrate toward being more like a Giver to be loving enough to let the Dreamer have a little of his or her territory back.

If you are a Dreamer with a Dominant partner, you can have great sex when the Dreamer can match his or her dream to the Dominant's worldview of control and certainty.

Elegants

Elegants are proper, rules-driven, and orderly, driven by fairness and consistency with natural law. They are well-groomed, well-dressed, and well-put-together inside and out. They can be rigid and inflexible in life, in business, and in bed, and this unyieldingness can be stressful to their relationship mates. Their key Facet of Sexual Expression is Fidelity.

What the Elegant Needs

Elegants need order, organization, neatness, and consistency with natural law. They are sensitive to clutter, both physical and also mental/emotional clutter. But they also reject philosophical clutter, preferring their version of spirituality, which governs much of their personal decision-making. Elegants, then, also need ethical consistency with their worldview.

How the Elegant Sees His/Her Partner

The Elegant sees his or her partner as a VIP, to be treated with dignity and respect. The Elegant has cultured manners and a professional approach to relationship, so his or her partner is revered unless they prove inconsistent with the Elegant's expectations, in which case they plummet in status and may even be vilified. The "fire and brimstone" orientation yields a black and white decision-making process that is more based on universal principles than with the Dominant, whose rules are personally inspired.

How the Elegant Interacts With the Other Types

Elegants are pristine in their self-management, with high standards for themselves and for how they judge others. So, it takes a lot to pass muster with an Elegant lover. The opposite is also true. Many Elegants have trouble in relationship since it's hard to measure up to their perfectionism.

Elegant-Elegant: The double Elegant couple has a highly developed rules structure. Both have stiff filters that determine what is acceptable, in bed and otherwise, and only behaviors and habits that work for both of them will be sustained in the relationship. Things get more fun when one or both integrate toward showing up more like a Player, enthusiastic, playful, and passionate. Elegants have that in them, but it is only expressed when they are at their healthiest.

If you are an Elegant with an Elegant partner, you can have great sex when one Elegant or both grow toward Player behaviors, and rides the flexibility and adventurousness to ecstasy.

Elegant-Giver: The Elegant will demonstrate rules and beliefs that stem from his or her interpretation of spirituality, and the Giver is likely to be supportive and helpful. So, Elegant-Giver couples are usually defined by the ideas and self-concept of the Elegant, with the Giver doing everything possible to help. As the Elegant grows toward being more like a Player, the adventurousness and fun are also supported by the Giver, but it's a better time overall. The more passionate and celebratory the Elegant becomes, the more the Giver is inspired to serve those outcomes in any way possible.

If you are an Elegant with a Giver partner, you can have great sex when the Elegant integrates and shows up more like a Player, and the Giver offers him or herself unconditionally to that series of adventures.

Elegant-Star: Because the Star can be so superficial and the Elegant so substantial, there can be a disconnection between the Star's self-absorption and the Elegant's perception of universal values. The Elegant may perceive the Star as shallow, while the Star may perceive the Elegant as overly serious, stiff, or stuffy. But when the Elegant grows to be more like a Player, it's easier for the Star to relate to the fun and passion.

If you are an Elegant with a Star partner, you can have great sex when the Elegant supports the Star's self-image, either from a place of natural rightness or by integrating towards showing up more like a Player, demonstrating more enthusiasm and playfulness.

Elegant-Romantic: When Elegants stress, they look more like stressed Romantics, and when Romantics grow, they look more like Elegants. So, in the Elegant-Romantic couple, the Elegant must remain the stronger, so the Romantic tends to integrate. But the real fun begins when the Elegant integrates toward being more like a Player, and the Romantic integrates toward being more like an Elegant. This starts to look like a healthy Player-Elegant couple, with the stability of the Elegant and the fun of the Player.

If you are an Elegant with a Romantic partner, you can have great sex when the Elegant grows to show up more like a Player, and the Romantic grows to show up more like an Elegant, leading to fun and passion with a tone of natural rightness.

Elegant-Professor: Elegants and Professors can have profound conversations about cosmic philosophy, or can argue over the right way to kiss—both are deeply convicted in their beliefs and worldviews. The best sexual atmosphere is generated when the Elegant integrates toward being more like a Player, becoming more flexible and relaxed. Then the Professor will feel less challenged by the precision and orderliness of the Elegant, though he or she will have to remain strong to avoid stressing toward Player energy. The Professor can apply his or her intellect without philosophical debate, and he or she can grow more easily toward being like a Dominant, whose big energy can both lead and inspire the evolving Elegant.

If you are an Elegant with a Professor partner, you can have great sex when the Elegant explores his or her integrative type, the Player, making him or her more fun and more likely to find adventure in the systems and distinctions of the Professor.

Elegant-Thinker: Elegants and Thinkers both carefully consider their options, but for different reasons. The Elegant is making an effort to remain consistent with natural law, while the Thinker is attempting to stay safe by noticing every possible danger. This makes the Elegant-Thinker couple cautious about sexuality, preferring to stay within safe and acceptable boundaries. But when the Elegant grows toward being more like a Player, and the Thinker grows toward being more like a Dreamer, the shackles come off, and they can experience a more expansive and entertaining sex life.

If you are an Elegant with a Thinker partner, you can have great sex when the Elegant integrates to show up more like a Player, and the Thinker integrates to show up more like a Dreamer, to make it more fun and more transcendent.

Elegant-Player: The Elegant grows by becoming more like a Player, so the Elegant-Player couple is a great fit, as long as the Player remains the stronger, influencing the Elegant to become more playful and flexible. If the Elegant is stronger, the Player will disintegrate toward being more like an Elegant, will stress over the limitations, and will probably leave or self-destruct. So, the ticket to sexual fulfillment in the Elegant-Player relationship is for the Player to be strong, and the Elegant to grow toward him or her.

If you are an Elegant with a Player partner, you can have great sex when the Player is stronger and the Elegant grows toward the Player, becoming more playful, flexible, passionate, and fun.

Elegant-Dominant: Elegants and Dominants both tend to be angry, but for different reasons. The Elegant is angry because of all the injustice and imperfections in the world, including sexually, while the Dominant uses the power of anger as a weapon to increase control. So, the Elegant-Dominant couple has great capacity for passion, especially if they learn how to channel their conflicts into constructive efforts. The challenge is that the "my rules for you, no rules for me" worldview of the Dominant may be in direct opposition to the rules structure of the Elegant, no less highly developed, but based more on natural rightness and universal law than the personal tastes of the Dominant. When these rules don't match up, it can be a fatal flaw in the relationship, so Elegants and Dominants must get together and define such rules and beliefs to get them into alignment. When they do, the potential for success is greatly increased. Also, as the Dominant integrates to become more like a Giver, love is offered more unconditionally than is typical for the stressing Dominant. Likewise for the Elegant—the growth toward being more like a Player offers additional flexibility and options the average Elegant may not have access to.

If you are an Elegant with a Dominant partner, you can have great sex when the Elegant is clear about boundaries and rules, and the Dominant is willing to be flexible enough to include them. When the Dominant shows up more like a Giver, and the Elegant shows up more like a Player, there can be loving fun that fulfills both.

Elegant-Dreamer: The Elegant-Dreamer couple usually follows the format desired by the Elegant, since the Dreamer is least likely to force his or her opinion onto the other. So, the Elegant will usually impose his or her boundaries, and the Dreamer will comply, up to a point. When the Dreamer's passive-aggressive behaviors start to bother the Elegant, there can be discussion and reformulation of the sexual guidelines, allowing more latitude for the Dreamer to get his or her fantasies considered and included. This happens more easily when the Elegant integrates toward being more like a Player, allowing for more flexibility and fun, which generally is enough to keep the Dreamer happy.

If you are an Elegant with a Dreamer partner, you can have great sex when the Elegant makes space for the Dreamer's fantasies, as long as they aren't too far over the top for the Elegant to handle. When the Elegant grows to show up more like a Player, the Dreamer frequently gets more latitude to express him or herself sexually, and things get even better.

In summary, each type of lover has particular patterns and idiosyncrasies, and a savvy relationship mate will learn his or her own patterns and the patterns of his or her partner, to improve the chances of great sex.

Points to Remember

1. Each type has values, standards and preferences that are either supported or hindered by the patterns of the partner. Any relationship can work if both partners understand these patterns and use them skillfully.

2. All types generally do better in the sexual aspects of their lives when they move in an integrative or healthy direction along the Sexual Wellness Line™.

Actions to Take

1. Identify your own type and the type of your partner, if you have one. (If you need more help with this, please see "The Nine Types Calculator," pages 89-92.)

2. Notice if you typically choose the patterns that improve connection, or those that reduce it. Choose a pattern you know works, and use it to be sure. Pick a pattern you suspect doesn't work, and eliminate it to see what happens next.

Questions to Ponder

What would happen if you and your partner selected constructive patterns of sexual connection and fulfillment?

What would happen if everyone did?

Sexuality is one of our great challenges, and also one of our great opportunities. You might think, what could be more natural? Yet it has been distorted in our culture to seem like something it is not. Hopefully, the content of this book will contribute to a change toward ecstasy, fulfillment, and sexual wellness. As this body of knowledge unfolds and expands, we can all look forward to good times, abundant love, healthful expression, and of course, great sex.

ACKNOWLEDGMENTS

Thank you, first of all, to my lovely wife, Regina, without whom none of this work would have been possible. Thanks also to my beautiful family; sons Jeremy, Sean, and Daniel, daughters-in-law Vanessa and Jamie, and granddaughter Sonja. And thanks to my dad, Dr. Bill Perman, and my late mom, Eileen Perman, may she rest in peace, for their unflagging support and enthusiasm.

Thank you to my mentors and teachers along the way, especially Anthony Robbins, whose ideas and technology contributed tremendously to all aspects of my growth and development. Thank you to my past and present business partners at The Masters Circle, Dr. Bob Hoffman and Dr. Larry Markson, whose input helped to shape my thinking. Thanks to Dr. Bob Bays for introducing me to the enneagram, and to Don Richard Riso and Russ Hudson for teaching me so much about it.

Thank you to Steve Harrison and Quantum Leap, my coaches and writing mentors, especially Geoffrey Berwind, Martha Bullen, and Brian Edmondson.

Thanks to Michael Gelb for being an inspiration and guide along the path of self-exploration and discovery, and to my longtime songwriting partner Mitch Clarvit for the use of the Perman~Clarvit song lyrics and for his unwavering faith in me.

Thanks to the editors at FirstEditing.com, and the great team at BookBaby.com for their support in producing this book.

And thanks, of course, to all the sexual pioneers who were courageous enough to push the envelope so more of us could have an experience of sexual wellness, which we all deserve and ultimately will all have.

ABOUT THE AUTHOR

Dr. Dennis Perman, healer, speaker, writer, coach, and entrepreneur, has been teaching wellness professionals for three decades. A graduate of Johns Hopkins University and New York Chiropractic College, he became infatuated with human behavior when he started studying with Anthony Robbins, rising to the level of Master Trainer, and lecturing extensively on communications techniques, leadership, social interaction, and relationships. His studies on NLP and the Enneagram led him to research sexuality, and You Can Have Great Sex *is his first book on the topic. You can read his blog at www.youcanhavegreatsex.com*

Future work will delve into sexual problem solving, optimizing your sexual technique, and advances in the psychology of sexual wellness. Look for "Ralph and Rebecca," a romance novel that applies the concepts of YCHGS, and from which excerpts have been interspersed throughout this book.

Dennis is happily married to the lovely Regina, and has three terrific sons, Jeremy, Sean, and Daniel; two wonderful daughters-in-law, Vanessa and Jamie; and a beautiful granddaughter, Sonja.

You can contact Dennis through Sexual Wellness Press,
631-742-7571, or email him at dennis@sexualwellnesspress.com.

.